ESL

50 ENGAGING ROLE PLAYS

ROLE

FOR ESL AND EFL CLASSES

PLAYS

Cover designed by Sherwin Soy

Discussion questions were used with the permission of ESL Conversation Questions
www.eslconversationquestions.com

Published by ECQ Publishing

Printed in the United States of America

First Printing, 2015

ISBN-10: 1942116071
ISBN-13: 978-1-942116-07-3

Distributed by
CreateSpace
4900 LaCross Road
North Charleston, SC 29406
USA
www.createspace.com/pub/l/createspacedirect.do

First Edition

TABLE OF CONTENTS

TABLE OF CONTENTS

Introduction

ESL Role Plays was written as a resource book for teachers of English as a foreign language. The role plays are designed to be flexible and can be used to support a number of different teaching styles. They are designed to supplement your lessons but many of the role plays can serve as standalone lessons for one or two hour classes.

Levels

The role plays included in this book will be most useful for teachers with intermediate to advanced students. While some role plays can be adapted to suit the needs of beginner students, they were made for intermediate to advanced learners of English.

Class Size

These role plays were created to be as flexible as possible in terms of class size. While the optimal class sizes for these role plays are eight to twenty four students, almost all of the role plays can be used with classes as small as three students or as large as necessary. For classes with over thirty students the core role play activity will work but the warm up and wrap up might need to be adjusted.

Role Play Contents

Included in each role play is a sample lesson plan for the teacher, discussion questions, and question cards or an activity sheet to be used with the role play.

Lesson plan

Teachers can decide what to include or omit from the lesson plan based on the needs of their class and time restraints. The full lesson can be done for a longer activity or just the core role play for a shorter activity.

Discussion questions

The discussion questions included in each role play are completely optional and can be added to any part of the lesson or completely ignored based on the needs of the teacher.

The discussion questions come from eslconversationquestions.com and some were questions were used in *1000 Conversation Questions: Designed for Use in the ESL or EFL Classroom*. So if you already have that book or frequent the website you may recognize some of the questions.

Question card / activity sheets

Included at the end of each role play are question cards or activity sheets for use during the role play. For most role plays with question cards, the cards will need to be copied and cut out for students. For role plays that use an activity sheet, copying and cutting out of the activity sheet is usually optional as students can fill in the same information on their own sheets of paper.

Topic Index

The role plays are listed by topic in the table of contents but many of the role plays can be applicable to a variety of topics. The topic index is a way for teachers to find role plays that are related to the topic of their lesson, even if the title of the role play doesn't appear to be related. If you can't find what you are looking for in the table of contents try the topic index.

ROLE

PLAYS

Adoption Role Play

Lesson Plan

Description - Students try to convince adoption agencies that they will be a good parent.

Preparation - Copy / cut role play cards before class. Prepare one role play card per student.

Warm up

Divide students into groups of three. A group of two or four can be made if necessary. For small classes, pair up students. Elicit traits or habits that make someone a good parent. Ask groups to brainstorm several questions an adoption agency might ask a person who is trying to adopt a child. Ask groups for their ideas and write some of their questions on the board.

Note - The discussion questions are about adoption in general, not just the adoption process. Depending on the teacher's preference, the discussion questions can be used during the warm up, wrap up, or as a supplement if the activity runs short.

Set up

Pair two students from each group of three and tell them they are a married couple trying to adopt a child. Alternatively, if you have a small class with pairs, tell one student in each pair that they are a potential parent trying to adopt. Tell the other student in the group that they will screen the adoption candidate for an adoption agency.

Hand the potential parents a role card and tell them to come up with reasons why they would be great parents. If they have a partner, tell them to discuss this together. Tell them they can use their imagination and create identities.

Hand the adoption agency employees their cards and tell them they should brainstorm what questions to ask and what they are looking for in order to allow parents to adopt.

Explain any unfamiliar vocabulary from the cards, i.e., potential parents, initial, adoption process, identity, etc.

Tell the adoption agency interviewers that they will only choose one set of parents as successful applicants to go to the next round of the adoption process. Encourage them to ask follow up questions and dig deep to make sure the people they are interviewing will be good parents.

Role play

Have all the students stand up and set up the desks so that the interviewers are facing the potential parents. Have all the parents sit facing the same way so they are facing the interviewer in their group. Next, rotate the potential parents clockwise so they are facing a new interviewer.

The potential parents will have four minutes to convince interviewers that they will be great parents. After four minutes, tell potential parents to rotate clockwise to the interviewer next to them and repeat. Repeat this for four turns or until they get back to their original group.

Wrap up

After the role play finishes, ask the parents to come to front of the class. Then, ask each interviewer which potential parent / couple they chose and why.

Discussion Questions

- How is adoption viewed in your country?

- Do you know anyone who was adopted? Can you think of any famous people who were adopted?

- How does being adopted affect a child's view of themselves?

- What are some of the reasons people adopt children?

- What are some of the reasons people give children up for adoption?

- What do you think about the adoption system in your country?

- What do you think about couples that adopt children from different countries?

- Should the adoption process be more, or less, difficult than it is now?

- Should people be able to decide what type of children they want to adopt? For example: boy or girl, hair color, age, etc.

- Should there be a limit on how many children a family can adopt?

- Should individuals be able to adopt, or should only married couples be able to adopt?

ADOPTION

Role Play Cards

Role 1
The adoption agency interviewer

You are in charge of choosing which potential parents get to adopt a child.

You work for an adoption agency. It's your job to interview potential parents and decide if they will make good parents. You are doing initial interviews to see which parents will go on to the next step in the adoption process. Remember, you are responsible for making sure children get put into a loving and happy home. You decide the future of each child you find a home for. Ask lots of good questions and follow up questions to find out if the potential parents will make good parents.

Role 2
The potential parent

You really want to be a parent, so you are trying adopt a child.

Use your imagination and create a new identity. Be the best parent ever. Create an identity the adoption agency interviewers will want to pick. Show the interviewers that you will be a great parent. Think of traits that make a good parent and create an identity around those traits. Remember, it's your dream to adopt a child, raise them in a great environment, and give them a great life.

Advice Role Play

Lesson Plan

Description - Students go to different life coaches to get advice about various problems they have.

Preparation - Make a copy of the "Problem Sheet" for every student. Find a picture of someone and brainstorm several problems you can say they have, i.e., bad work life balance, eating unhealthy snacks because they are busy, wanting to meet a girlfriend / boyfriend.

Warm up

Show a picture of a person to the class. Tell the class the problems that you have created for the person. Explain that a life coach is someone who gives advice on how a person can improve their life. Ask students to pretend they are life coaches and the person has come to them for help. What advice would they give them?

Note - The discussion questions are about advice in general, not about life coaches. Depending on the teacher's preference, the discussion questions can be used during the warm up, wrap up, or as a supplement if the activity runs short.

Set up

Tell students they are going to visit a life coach to help them with their problems.

Give each student in the class a "Problem Sheet". Tell them to write two or three problems they are facing in their life. Emphasize that they SHOULD NOT make their problems extremely personal or embarrassing since they will be sharing the problems with other students. Really emphasize this or you will have some students sharing uncomfortable details about themselves. Let them know they can make up problems if they don't want to share their actual problems.

Give students time to write their problems down.

Divide the class in half. Half of the students will be life coaches and the other half will be customers. If there is an odd number of students, make two students a life coach team.

Role play

Have all the students stand up and set up the desks with one desk facing another. Have all the life coaches sit facing the same way so they have an empty seat in front of them. Next, let all the customers sit down in front of a life coach of their choice.

1st Round

They will have three minutes to talk about their problems and get advice. After three minutes, tell customers to rotate clockwise to the life coach next to them and get different advice for three minutes. Repeat this for four turns or until students get back to their original life coach.

2nd Round

After the 1st round, customers and life coaches switch roles. Life coaches will pull out their problems sheet and become customers. After they switch roles, customers rotate around just like in the 1st round.

Wrap up

After each round, ask a few students if they received any advice that they will actually take. If they say yes, ask them what the advice was and who gave it to them.

Discussion Questions

- What three pieces of advice will you give your children?

- Whose advice do you follow more, your parents' or your friends' advice?

- If you could give the leader of your country some advice, what would it be?

- If you could go back in time and give yourself some advice, what would you tell your younger self?

- Who was the wisest person in your country's history? What kind of advice did they give?

- Where do you go to get good advice?

- What are some things students should do to improve their English?

- What should I do to make more money?

- What should people do when first meeting their boyfriend / girlfriend's parents?

- What should someone do to be happy?

Problem Sheet

Problems

Visiting a life coach

You are going to visit many life coaches to get advice for your problems.

Remember, don't list problems that are too personal or are potentially embarrassing. If all of your problems are too personal or embarrassing, you can make up problems.

Some examples of possible problems: difficult to stay motivated, want to exercise more, want to learn a skill but don't have enough time, want to eat healthier, etc.

Your problems:

- _____

- _____

- _____

Notes:

_____
_____
_____
_____
_____
_____
_____

Aliens Role Play

Lesson Plan

Description - The UN has decided that it wants to make the search for alien life a priority. A group has been formed to decide the best way to search for alien life.

Preparation - Copy / cut role play cards before class. Prepare one role play card per student.

Warm up

Divide the class into groups of four. A group of three can be made if necessary. Write these questions on the board: "What are the possible pros and cons of humans finding intelligent alien life?", "What are the possible pros and cons of humans finding non-intelligent alien life?" Let students discuss and then elicit some ideas after they have finished.

Note – The discussion questions are about aliens in general, not just about the search for aliens. Depending on the teacher's preference, the discussion questions can be used during the warm up, wrap up, or as a supplement if the activity runs short.

Set up

Tell the class that the UN is going to expand the search for alien life. The UN has formed a group to decide on the best way to search for alien life. They are that group.

Hand each student in the group a role play card and give them time to read it. If you have a group of three, you can take out role card four. Tell students they shouldn't show their group members their card. Explain any unfamiliar vocabulary from the cards, i.e., probe, radio waves, hostile, rover, colonize,

bacterial / viral life, etc. Give the students time to prepare their arguments.

Explain that by the end of the role play they must have a recommendation to give to the UN. There can be some compromise, but there isn't enough funding to do all of the methods. There is only enough funding to do one method really well.

Role play

Students can stay seated in their groups. All groups in the class will do the role play at the same time while the teacher monitors and makes notes of common errors. Try not to interrupt or interfere with the role play unless absolutely necessary.

Give students around ten minutes to complete the role play. The role play may run short or long depending on how outgoing and confident your students are.

Once it looks like one or two of the groups are finishing up, give the other groups two minutes to finish up their role plays and come to a decision.

Wrap up

After students finish, ask each group their recommendation and why they chose that method to recommend.

Discussion Questions

- Do you believe there is other life in the universe? How about intelligent life?

- What do you think aliens might look like?

- Do you think aliens have ever visited earth?

- What does UFO mean?

- Have you seen a UFO or do you know someone who has seen a UFO?

- What is your favorite alien from a movie?

- What is the scariest alien movie?

- If aliens did come to a country and met with the government of that country, what do you think would happen?

- Why are humans so fascinated by aliens?

- How many planets do you think are in our galaxy? How about the universe?

- Do you think humans will travel to another planet in your lifetime?

- How do you think we or aliens will get to other star systems like our own? (If we traveled at the speed of light, the nearest star with planets that we know of is 10.5 years away.)

ALIENS

Role Play Cards

Role 1
Send a message to the aliens.

You want to send a message to aliens using different technologies.

The best way to find aliens is to send a message to them. Once we let them know that we are here, they can contact us or visit us with their advanced technology. We have already been sending out television and radio waves into space, but we need to try other technologies, like lasers, to contact the aliens. Maybe they don't use radio waves to communicate. Your goal is to convince the group to send messages into space to find aliens.

Role 2
Listen for the aliens.

You want to listen for aliens in more places and use different technologies

The best way to find aliens is to listen for them. If they want to be contacted or want to help other life forms, they will send out a message. We need to figure out how to listen for that message. We've been trying to find them by searching for radio waves, but we've only searched a tiny part of the sky. We need to expand the search and try different technologies for listening. It's dangerous to send out messages. What if the aliens hear our message and they are hostile? Your goal is to convince the group to listen for aliens.

Role 3
Search for simple alien life in our solar system.

You want to search for simple alien life like bacteria but in our own solar system.

We shouldn't waste money on searching for distant aliens when we haven't even searched our own solar system yet. We need to send probes and rovers to different planets in our own solar system to search for life. If we find bacterial or viral life on another planet or moon in our solar system it means there is alien life farther out in space. Plus, we don't know what would happen if we came into contact with another intelligent life form. It could be terrible for humans. There is also a greater chance that this way will be successful. Your goal is to convince the group to send probes and rovers around our solar system first.

Role 4
Colonize space and find aliens later.

You want to send humans to other planets. We might or might not find alien life, but either way, we will have colonized another planet.

Searching for alien life is good, but what if we don't find it? Even if alien life is out there, we might not find it. We should colonize Mars and worry about searching for life when we get there. Even if we don't find alien life on Mars, we will still have a colony there and will learn a lot about other worlds and colonizing other planets. We can worry about finding aliens as we colonize our own solar system.

Animals Role Play

Lesson Plan

Description - Employees of an NGO try to decide which endangered animal to focus on. Each student will argue for a different animal.

Preparation - Make a copy of the "Endangered Animal Sheet" for each student. Prepare pictures of endangered animals.

Warm up

Show students pictures of endangered animals. Elicit more animals that are endangered. Write them on the board. Ask students why some of the animals are endangered.

Note- The discussion questions focus on animals in general, not just endangered animals. Depending on the teacher's preference, the discussion questions can be used during the warm up, wrap up, or as a supplement if the activity runs short.

Set up

Divide the class into groups of three. A group of two or four can be created if necessary. Give individual students one or two minutes to choose an endangered animal. They can choose one from the board, from the pictures, one they heard about before, or one they found online. After the two minutes is up, ask them to check with their group members to make sure no one else chose their animal. Explain to students what an NGO is.

Give students eight minutes to complete the "Endangered Animal Sheet". Allow them to use their phones or laptops to research more about their animals.

After they have finished filling in the sheet, tell the students they are employees of an NGO that helps save endangered animals. The NGO needs to decide which animal to focus on next to try and save. Each group member has an endangered animal to propose to the group. The group will need to choose which animal to help and then decide how they will help that animal.

Role play

Students should arrange their desks so they are facing each other. All groups in the class will do the role play at the same time while the teacher monitors and makes notes of common errors. Try not to interrupt or interfere with the role play unless absolutely necessary.

Give each group around seven minutes to choose an animal to help. When one or two groups have come to a decision as to what animal to try and save, let the other groups know they have two minutes to choose which animal to help.

Then, give the groups about eight minutes to brainstorm ideas about how to help save the animal they chose. The role play may run short or long depending on how outgoing and confident your students are.

Wrap up

Have each group present the animal they chose and how they plan to help that animal.

Discussion Questions

- What animal best represents you? Why?

- What creature scares you? Why?

- Except for food, do humans need other animals? Why or why not?

- What is the most effective way to save endangered species?

- What are some examples of useful traits that help animals survive? (i.e., a giraffe's long neck)

- What traits have made humans a successful species?

- What is the cutest animal you can think of? How about the ugliest?

- Why do humans have pets? Do you have a pet? Why or why not?

- Are there any animals that we should try to kill off completely?

- Are humans responsible for saving animals from extinction? Why or why not?

Endangered Animal Sheet

Endangered Animal
Save an endangered animal.

You are going to choose an endangered animal for your NGO to focus on and then convince your fellow NGO employees to select your animal.

Remember, you can choose any endangered animal you want, but you must support your opinion with reasons why your animal is so important.

Animal information:

- Name of animal: _____

- Where it lives: _____

More details about the animal:
(Why should your NGO focus on saving this animal? Why is it endangered? Is there a good chance of being able to save the animal?)

_____

_____

_____

_____

_____

_____

_____

_____

_____

_____

_____

_____

Art Role Play

Lesson Plan

Description - Artists try to convince a curator to put their strange art in a gallery.

Preparation - Copy / cut role play cards before class. Prepare one role play card per student. Find pictures of strange or silly modern art for the warm up. Some recent art can easily be found by searching "strange modern art" online.

Warm up

Show pictures of the modern art you found online. Put students in groups of three. Groups of two can be made if necessary. Ask them to talk about what they think of the modern art you showed them. Then, elicit whether they think it's actually art. Finally, ask groups to try to come up with a definition of art without looking in their dictionary. Elicit their definitions.

Note - The discussion questions are about art in general, not just about modern art. Depending on the teacher's preference, the discussion questions can be used during the warm up, wrap up, or as a supplement if the activity runs short.

Set up

Tell groups that one of them in the group will be an art gallery curator who must choose which artist to include in their next exhibition. The other students in the group will be artists. For groups of two, the curator must choose whether or not to accept the artist's art in the next exhibition.

Hand each student in the group a role play card and give them time to read it. If you have a group of two, you can use the two member group role play cards. Tell students they shouldn't show their group members their card. Explain any unfamiliar vocabulary from the cards.

Give the artists time to think about what they will say about their art. Give curators time to think about how they will choose the artist.

Explain that the curator must choose one of the artists' art to put in the show at the end of the role play. If you have a group of two, it's up to the curator to decide whether or not to include the art. At the end of the role play, they'll tell the artist whether or not they'll accept the art.

Role play

Students can stay seated or do their role play standing up. All groups in the class will do the role play at the same time while the teacher monitors and makes notes of common errors. Try not to interrupt or interfere with the role play unless absolutely necessary.

Give students around eight minutes to complete the role play. The role play may run short or long depending on how outgoing and confident your students are.

Once it looks like one or two of the groups are finishing up, give the other groups one or two minutes to finish up their role plays.

Wrap up

Ask each curator their decision and why they chose the artist. For groups of two, ask if they decided to accept the artist's art and why.

Discussion Questions

- How often do you go to art museums?

- Do you consider yourself to be artistic?

- What do you think about modern art paintings?

- How many forms of art can you name? What is your favorite form of art?

- Is graffiti art? Why or why not?

- What is the most famous statue in your country?

- Who is your favorite artist? Why do you like them so much?

- Do you think that art is important to society? Why?

- Have you ever tried drawing, painting, sculpting, or something else artistic?

- What is the most famous painting in your country?

- What is traditional art like in your culture?

- What country do you think is the most creative?

- Why is art so expensive? Do you think it should be more, or less, expensive?

- Do you have any artistic friends? What kinds of art do they create?

ART

Role Play Cards

Role 1
The curator

You are the curator of an art gallery. You must choose between two pieces of art for your next art exhibition.

You run an art gallery, and one of your artists pulled out of the exhibition at the last moment. You don't have much time before the exhibition, so you must choose between these two unknown artists. Their art looks very similar. Both of their art pieces look like trash from the street glued onto a canvas. You don't like their art, but you need to have something to replace the artist who pulled out of the exhibition. Your goal is to choose between the two artists.

Role 2
Artist one

You are an artist. Convince the art curator to choose your art piece.

You have been working on this piece of art for months. The trash from the street that you glued on the canvas was carefully chosen. Each piece of trash represents a part of the human body. The art piece shows that humans are disposable, just like the products we make. Even though we think we are special, other humans use us and throw us away. This art exhibit is your chance to finally become a successful artist. The problem is that the other artist has a very similar art piece to yours. Your goal is to convince the art curator to choose your art.

Role 3
Artist two

You are not an artist. Convince the art curator to choose your art piece.

Your friend told you that if you could get some trash put into an art gallery he would give you $2,000. You thought it would be fun to try, so you looked at some art galleries and found one that was accepting art submissions. Yesterday, you picked up some trash from the street and glued it to a canvas. Now you have an interview with the art curator. The funny thing is, another person brought some trash on a canvas as well. Your goal is to make up reasons why your art is special and should be chosen to be put into the art gallery.

Group of two cards

You are the curator of an art gallery. You must choose whether to accept this artist's art into your art exhibition.

You run an art gallery, and one of your artists cancelled at the last moment. You don't have much time before the exhibition, so you must find a new artist quickly. You put a sign up asking for submissions, and this artist was the first and only one to contact you. Their art looks like they glued trash on a piece of canvas. You don't know if any other artists will contact you, and your exhibition is tomorrow. You must choose whether to accept this artist's art or not.

You are not an artist. Convince the art curator to choose your art piece.

Your friend told you that if you could get some trash put into an art gallery he would give you $2,000. You thought it would be fun to try, so you looked at some art galleries and found one that was accepting art submissions. Yesterday, you picked up some trash from the street and glued it to a canvas. Now you have an interview with the art curator. Your goal is to make up reasons why your art is special and should be chosen to be put into the art gallery.

Books Role Play

Lesson Plan

Description - Bookstore owners must decide what books to stock with their limited budget.

Preparation - Copy / cut role play cards before class. Prepare one role play card per student.

Warm up

Divide students into groups of three. A group of two can be made if necessary. Ask groups to come up with examples of popular fiction books, non-fiction books, and serious literary fiction. Tell them to discuss what they think of each category. Elicit some of their examples and thoughts.

Note - The discussion questions are about books in general, not about bookstores. Depending on the teacher's preference, the discussion questions can be used during the warm up, wrap up, or as a supplement if the activity runs short.

Set up

Tell students they are the new owners of a bookstore café. They must decide what types of books they want to stock their bookstore with. They have a budget of $20,000 to buy books. Write $20,000 on the board. If you have a group of two, let them know they have $15,000 dollars.

Hand each student in the group a role play card and give them time to read it. If you have a group of two, you can leave out role card three. Tell students they shouldn't show their group members their card. Explain any unfamiliar vocabulary from the cards. Give students time to think of arguments for their role.

Remind them that the group must come to a decision by the end of the role play.

Role play

Students should arrange their desks so they are facing each other. All groups in the class will do the role play at the same time while the teacher monitors and makes notes of common errors. Try not to interrupt or interfere with the role play unless absolutely necessary.

Give students around eight minutes to complete the role play. The role play may run short or long depending on how outgoing and confident your students are.

When one or two groups have come to a decision, let the other groups know they have two minutes to finish up.

Wrap up

Elicit from each group how they decided to split the money and why they decided to split it that way.

Discussion Questions

- Do you read many books?

- How often do you read books?

- Did your parents read to you when you were a child?

- What are some of the advantages of books vs. movies? How about the disadvantages of books vs. movies?

- What was the last book you read?

- Do you prefer fiction or non-fiction books?

- Do you think people don't read enough books these days?

- If you could only read one more book for your entire life, what would it be?

- Can a book change the world?

- Who is an author that you like? Why do you like their books?

- What is one example of traditional literature in your country? Did you have to read it in school?

- Do you like reading the traditional literature of your country?

Role Play Cards

Role 1

Popular fiction

You think popular fiction will make the most money for the bookstore.

You think the best use of the money is to stock the store with as many best seller fiction books as possible. If you stock popular fiction books, people will buy more of those books. Plus, if people read the books while sitting in the café, they will spend even more money. Sure, some of the books are just entertainment and not intellectually stimulating, but we should give the people what they want. Your goal is to spend $15,000 on popular fiction books, if possible. But no less than $10,000.

Role 2

Non-fiction

You think non-fiction will make the most money for the bookstore.

You think the money would be best spent on non-fiction books. People use non-fiction books for reference, so they will want a physical book. If people want to buy popular fiction, they usually buy the ebook, not the physical book. If we buy non-fiction books, people won't just sit around reading without buying anything. They'll see the non-fiction book they want, buy it, and go. You think the store will make a lot more money with non-fiction books. Your goal is to spend $15,000 on non-fiction books, if possible. But no less than $10,000.

Role 3

Serious literary fiction

You think the bookstore should be for intelligent people who love literature.

You don't want to own a bookstore to make a huge amount of money. You want to own a bookstore because you love books. You want to attract other people who love books. The big bookstores went out of business because they focused only on making a profit. It's better for a small bookstore to develop loyal customers who love books. If we buy popular fiction and non-fiction books because we think we will make money, we'll go out of business. They can buy those at a cheaper price online. Customers should come to our bookstore because they know we love books. Your goal is to spend $15,000 on serious literary fiction, if possible. But no less than $10,000.

Camping Role Play

Lesson Plan

Description - Friends go camping and argue about when to come back.

Preparation - Copy / cut role play cards before class. Prepare one role play card per student. Find some photos of wilderness that your students will set their role play in.

Warm up

Divide students into groups of three. A group of two can be made if necessary. Ask students to brainstorm some of the good and bad things about camping. Have them write their ideas on the board in two columns.

Note - The discussion questions are about camping in general. Depending on the teacher's preference, the discussion questions can be used during the warm up, wrap up, or as a supplement if the activity runs short.

Set up

Tell students they are friends on a camping trip. They are camping far away from civilization. Show them the photos you found and tell them this is where they are camping.

Hand each student in the group a role play card and give them time to read it. If you have a group of two you can leave out role card three. Tell students they shouldn't show their group members their card. Explain any unfamiliar vocabulary from the cards. Give students time to think of arguments to support their role.

Explain that whatever the group chooses to do, they must do it together. It's dangerous to be alone so far from civilization.

Role play

Students can stay seated in a group or do their role play standing up. If you really wanted to make it more realistic, you could have them sit on the ground.

All groups in the class will do the role play at the same time while the teacher monitors and makes notes of common errors. Try not to interrupt or interfere with the role play unless absolutely necessary.

Give students around eight minutes to complete the role play. The role play may run short or long depending on how outgoing and confident your students are.

When one or two groups have come to a decision, tell the rest of the groups they have one minute to come to a decision about what to do.

Wrap up

Ask each group to tell the class what they decided to do and why.

Discussion Questions

- How many times have you gone camping? Did you enjoy it?

- Where have you gone camping?

- What are the four most important things to bring when you go camping?

- Is camping with lots of amenities (solar panels, fans, stove, etc.) still camping?

  How much luxury is too much?

- Where is the best place to go camping in your country?

- What is the longest time you have spent camping?

- Tell a story about a camping trip (it doesn't have to be your story).

- What is the best thing about camping? How about the worst thing?

- What is the best food to bring on a camping trip?

- What is the best activity to do while camping?

CAMPING

Role Play Cards

Role 1
Nature lover

You and your friends are on a camping trip. Everyone needs to agree on when to go back.

You are having a great time. You love being out in nature. You and your friends agreed to stay out camping for a week, but it's only been two days, and one of your friends already wants to go back. You think your friend will get used being out in nature and start to enjoy it eventually. Everyone came in your truck, so they can't go back unless you agree to, and you don't want to go back. Your goal is to get everyone to agree to stay at least a week and longer, if possible.

Role 2
Missing the city

You and your friends are on a camping trip. Everyone needs to agree on when to go back.

You are having a HORRIBLE time. You're getting bitten by insects. Your allergies are acting up. You are sure you are going to get sick from drinking the water out here. You want to go back to the city right now. You definitely don't want to stay for the rest of the week. You've already been here two days, and you don't want to spend another minute here. But you can't leave because your friend drove you out here. Your goal is to leave as soon as possible.

Role 3
Peacemaker

You and your friends are on a camping trip. Everyone needs to agree on when to go back.

You are having an okay time. You like camping, but the main reason you came out is to spend time with your friends. However, your friends are fighting about how long to stay. Camping isn't fun if both of your friends are fighting. You need to stop the fighting, or this is going to be a horrible trip. Your goal is to get your friends to stop arguing and get them to agree on how long to stay. You don't care what they decide on as long as they stop fighting and starting having fun.

Challenges Role Play

Lesson Plan

Description - Contestants are applying to be on a new reality adventure show where they will go on challenging adventures.

Preparation – Copy / cut one "Interview Sheet" and one "Contestant sheet" for each student. Gather pictures, stories, or video clips of people going on challenging adventures (optional).

Warm up

Divide the class into groups of three or four. Present the pictures, stories, or video clips of people attempting different difficult challenges (climbing Everest, sailing alone across the Pacific, diving in Antarctica, doing some insane trick on a bike, etc.), if you prepared them. Ask them to brainstorm some other stories or examples of people attempting difficult challenges. Go over some of their ideas as a class.

Note - The discussion questions are about challenges in general, not just about adventures. Depending on the teacher's preference, the discussion questions can be used during the warm up, wrap up, or as a supplement if the activity runs short.

Set up

Explain that contestants are being interviewed for a reality adventure show. The interviewer will choose one contestant to be the winner. The winning contestant will receive $2,000,000 and go on challenging adventures. The contestants must show they have the experience and skills to handle the challenges they will face on the show.

Hand one student in each group an interview sheet and give the rest of the students in the group a contestant sheet. Give the students time to read it. Explain any unfamiliar vocabulary. Give students five minutes to formulate questions, experiences, and skills.

Groups should arrange their desks or chairs to look like an interview, with the contestants' chairs facing the interviewer. Explain that the contestants will try to convince the interviewer to choose them for the show. At the end of the role play the interviewer will choose a winner.

Role play

All groups in the class will do the role play at the same time while the teacher monitors and makes notes of common errors. Try not to interrupt or interfere with the role play unless absolutely necessary.

Give students around eight minutes to complete the role play. The role play may run short or long depending on how outgoing and confident your students are. When two or three groups look like they are finished, end the role play.

Wrap up

For each group, ask the interviewer who they chose as the winning contestant and why.

Extension

The winner of each group can become the interviewer for the second season of the show, and the interviewers can become contestants. The contestants who didn't win can be mixed into different groups and then try again.

Discussion Questions

- What is a challenge you have faced?

- What kind of challenge would you like to try?

- Do you have any heroes that have done something amazing?

- Challenges don't have to be amazing. What are some normal challenges people face?

- Some people think that facing challenges improves a person. Do you agree or disagree?

- What are some challenges you think the next generation will face?

- Should people make their children have easy lives with few challenges or make sure their children face challenges?

- What are some modern challenges that humans must deal with in the present that humans didn't have to deal with in the past?

- What do you think makes some people seek out challenges and some people avoid them?

- What challenge are you most proud that you overcame?

CHALLENGES

Interview Sheet

Interviewer
Question sheet

You are an interviewer for a new adventure reality TV show. Your goal is to choose the best candidate for the show.

Interview the contestants. You are looking for someone who will be entertaining to watch, has overcome some difficult challenges, and has the necessary skills for the challenging adventures they will be doing on the show.

You have the feeling that some of the contestants are lying. You can try to catch them lying. Try to give all candidates equal time during the interview. You can cut off candidates if they are talking too long.

Some examples of the challenging adventures they might be doing on the show: surviving in the Amazon alone for two weeks, climbing mountains that no human has climbed before, hunting fish in shark filled waters with just a knife, or other crazy adventures that viewers submit.

QUESTIONS

- What experiences have prepared you for this TV show?

- What skills do you have that will be useful during the show?

-

-

-

-

-

-

-

-

Contestant Sheet

Contestant

Preparation sheet

You are a contestant for a new adventure reality TV show. Your goal is to be the one candidate that gets chosen.

You really need the $2,000,000. Plus, you are really excited to take on some of the challenging adventures that you'll go on.

You can lie, point out other contestants' lies, and do anything you need to do to get chosen. Don't be afraid to interrupt other contestants. You want to get the attention of the interviewer and have them choose you. If you want to be chosen, you'll have to stand out and be unique.

Some examples of the challenging adventures you might be doing: surviving in the Amazon alone for two weeks, climbing mountains that no human has climbed before, hunting fish in shark filled waters with just a knife, or other crazy adventures that viewers submit.

Previous experiences:
(i.e., survived for a year in the deserts of Africa, wrestled bears for exercise, etc.)

-

-

-

-

-

Skills
(i.e., hunting with just a stick, building shelters, swimming long distances, etc.)

_____

_____

_____

_____

_____

Charity Fundraising Role Play

Lesson Plan

Description – Students choose a charity and then must try to raise money for the charity from the other students.

Preparation – Make a copy of the "Charity Sheet" for each student (optional). Students will need to research and choose a charity. This can be done as homework or done in class on their phones.

Warm up

Put students in groups of four. Make a group of three or five if necessary. Ask groups to brainstorm some problems that charities try to solve. Groups should write their ideas on the board.

Ask groups to discuss which problems are the most serious and which can be fixed with enough effort or money.

Note - The discussion questions are about charities in general, not about raising money. Depending on the teacher's preference, the discussion questions can be used during the warm up, wrap up, or as a supplement if the activity runs short.

Set up

Tell students they are going to try to raise money for their favorite charity.

Give each student in class the "Charity Sheet", if you decide to use it. Tell the students to research and choose a charity on their phone if you didn't tell them to research a charity for homework. Give students time to find a charity and to fill in the charity sheet or make notes about their charity. Alternatively, students can make up a new charity, if you prefer.

When they are finished, or after ten minutes, divide the class into two lines facing each other. Half of the students will be fundraisers and the other half will be possible donors. If there is an odd number of students, have two students be a team.

Role play

Rotate the students once so they know how they will be rotating, i.e., each fundraiser move to their right with the last one in line going to the front. Let donors know they are going to donate $100 to just one charity. They can only choose one charity, so they should choose carefully.

1st Round

The fundraisers will have three minutes to convince the possible donor to make a donation. After three minutes, tell the fundraisers to rotate to the next donor. Repeat this for four turns or until students get back to their original partner. Then, rotate once more but don't let them ask for a donation. (This ensures that the person they just finished talking to isn't obliged to choose them.) Ask each donor what charity they will choose to donate to. Congratulate the two fundraisers who raised the most money.

2nd Round

For the 2nd round, the fundraisers will now be the donors. After switching roles, repeat the instructions from the 1st round.

Wrap up

After the role play, put students into groups of three or four and have them discuss what fundraising strategies worked best. Elicit some ideas.

Discussion Questions

- Do you give to charity or volunteer?

- What do you think are some important charities people should give to?

- Do you know of any bizarre charities?

- Do you give money to homeless people? Do you think people should give money to homeless people?

- Who do you think needs charity the most?

- How much do you think governments should give to help other countries?

- Should rich people and corporations be forced to give to charity? Is it charity if they are forced to give it?

- Do you think there are charities that are scams?

- Does your country have a holiday when it is traditional to help people in your community? If not, should there be a holiday like that?

- Do you think it is better to give time or money?

Charity Sheet

Charity

Why should people donate to your charity?

You are going to try to raise money for a charity of your choice.

Research a charity, and make notes about it and why it's important for people to donate to the charity.

Name of the charity:

* _____

Who the charity helps:

_____

_____

_____

_____

How the charity helps:

_____

_____

_____

_____

Why people should donate to the charity:

_____

_____

_____

_____

Cities Role Play

Lesson Plan

Description - City officials are trying to decide on what to do with a neighborhood in the city.

Preparation - Copy / cut role play cards before class. Prepare one role play card per student. Find pictures of famous cities (optional).

Warm up

Divide students into groups of three. A group of two can be made if necessary. Show groups the pictures of famous cities (if you prepared the pictures) and see which groups can guess which city it is. Ask students what they know about each city. Write this sentence on the board: "What makes a city great?" Have groups discuss and elicit some of their thoughts.

Note - The discussion questions are about cities in general. Depending on the teacher's preference, the discussion questions can be used during the warm up, wrap up, or as a supplement if the activity runs short.

Set up

Let students know they are city officials who must choose what to do with a neighborhood in their city. Each of them must convince the rest to choose their idea. The whole group must agree on one decision.

Hand each student in the group a role play card and give them time to read it. If you have a group of two you can leave out role card three. Tell students they shouldn't show their group members their card. Explain any unfamiliar vocabulary from the cards. Give students time to think of how they will present their argument.

Remind them they must come to a decision by the end of the role play.

Role play

Students should arrange their desks so they are facing each other. All groups in the class will do the role play at the same time while the teacher monitors and makes notes of common errors. Try not to interrupt or interfere with the role play unless absolutely necessary.

Give students around ten minutes to complete the role play. The role play may run short or long depending on how outgoing and confident your students are.

When one or two groups have come to a decision, let the other groups know they have two minutes to finish up.

Wrap up

Elicit from each group what they decided to do with the area and why they chose to do that.

Discussion Questions

- Do you like cities or the country side? Which is better and why?

- You can make one change to your country's capital, what will you change?

- What are some of most famous cities in the world? What makes them famous?

- Why do you think that humans started living in cities?

- Do you think we will still live in cities 100 years from now?

- How do you think cities will change in the future?

- What city would you like to visit?

- Are cities good for the environment or bad for the environment?

- What city is best known for:

    o fashion?

    o technology?

    o art?

    o industry?

    o travel?

Role Play Cards

Role 1

Build nice affordable housing.

You are a city official. You must decide on how to use six blocks of city land that will be cleared.

There are a lot of poor people living in the city. They live in apartments and houses that are falling apart, and there have been health problems because of the old buildings. You want to build a set of really nice affordable apartments that some of the poorer residents can move into. The government will pay for some of their rent so that the rent will be cheap enough. You think city officials have a duty to make sure all of the residents, rich or poor, have safe housing.

Role 2

Build a business district.

You are a city official. You must decide on how to use six blocks of city land that will be cleared.

You think the six blocks should be turned into a business district. This will attract new businesses which will mean more money for the city from taxes. It will also mean that the crime in the area will go down. Your goal is to turn the land into a center for business and trade. You think attracting new businesses to the city should be the number one goal of the city.

Role 3

Build a park.

You are a city official. You must decide on how to use six blocks of city land that will be cleared.

The city doesn't have many public spaces. You think the land should be used as a city park with a stage. If a park is built, it will dramatically improve the lives of people living near it and raise the property value of the homes and apartments near it. The stage in the park will also provide a place for artists to gather and perform. This will improve the cultural scene of the city and draw in more residents who have money.

Cleanliness Role Play

Lesson Plan

Description - Roommates argue about how clean their apartment should be.

Preparation - Copy / cut role play cards before class. Prepare one role play card per student.

Warm up

Divide students into groups of three. A group of two can be made if necessary. Write on the board: "How clean is too clean for a house or an apartment? How dirty is too dirty?"

Note - The discussion questions are about cleanliness in general, not just about dirty roommates. Depending on the teacher's preference, the discussion questions can be used during the warm up, wrap up, or as a supplement if the activity runs short.

Set up

Tell students they are roommates who have different views about cleanliness. You are all having an argument about how clean the apartment should be. Try to come to an agreement that makes everyone happy.

Hand each student in the group a role play card and give them time to read it. If you have a group of two you can leave out role card three. Tell students they shouldn't show their group members their card, but the dirty and clean roommate should identify who they are. Explain any unfamiliar vocabulary from the cards. Give students time to think of arguments to support their role.

Explain that whatever the roommates decide, they should all agree.

Role play

Students can stay seated in a group or do their role play standing up.

All groups in the class will do the role play at the same time while the teacher monitors and makes notes of common errors. Try not to interrupt or interfere with the role play unless absolutely necessary.

Give students around eight minutes to complete the role play. The role play may run short or long depending on how outgoing and confident your students are.

When one or two groups have come to an agreement that everyone is happy with, tell the rest of the groups they have one minute to come to an agreement about what to do.

Wrap up

Ask each group to tell the class what they agreed on and why.

Discussion Questions

- Did your mom let you get dirty when you were a child?

- What is the dirtiest you have ever been?

- How often do you clean your house or room?

- Do you do the dishes right after eating? How long do you let the dirty dishes sit without washing them?

- If you drop food on the floor, do you pick it up, blow on it, and eat it?

- What is the dirtiest job?

- How often do you wash your hands with soap?

- What is the grossest thing you have seen someone do?

- Who was the dirtiest person you ever met?

- Do you know anyone who is REALLY concerned about germs and cleanliness?

- How can bacteria help humans?

Role Play Cards

Role 1
The dirty roommate

Your roommate is really angry at you. You think they are overreacting.

One of your roommates is way too clean. Sure, you can be a little dirty sometimes, but it's not that bad. You think the apartment is clean enough. If they want it to be cleaner they can clean it themselves. It's mostly your room that is a little dirty, and your room is your business not theirs. You try to help out and clean up the common areas of the apartment like the living room and kitchen. You think you do a good job cleaning up. You think your clean roommate is a little crazy. Your goal is for everything to continue how it is and not make changes.

Role 2
The clean roommate

You are furious at your roommate. They're making the apartment disgusting.

Your roommate is incredibly disgusting! Your dirty roommate doesn't do their dishes and leaves them out until they grow mold. Their room is so dirty it spills out into the living room and makes the apartment stink. Your dirty roommate tries to clean sometimes but doesn't do it well. Your dirty roommate says you are better at cleaning, and if you have a problem with the apartment you should clean it. Their shower is so dirty you think they come out of the shower dirtier than when they went in. Your goal is to make the apartment a lot cleaner!

Role 3
The peacemaker

Your roommates are arguing. You don't care how clean or dirty the apartment is, you just want them to live together peacefully.

You have a dirty roommate and a clean roommate. You agree that the dirty roommate is definitely dirty, but you don't care about how clean the apartment is. You don't mind cleaning up more or you are fine with keeping it dirty, but you don't want to live with two people who are always arguing and fighting. Your goal is to help them come to an agreement that they can both live with.

Cloning Role Play

Lesson Plan

Description - Researchers try to convince a politician that cloning humans is a good / bad idea.

Preparation - Copy / cut role play cards before class. Prepare one role play card per student.

Warm up

Divide students into groups of three. A group of four can be made if necessary. Have groups brainstorm the pros and cons of cloning humans. Elicit some of their answers as a class.

Note - The discussion questions are about cloning humans and cloning in general. Depending on the teacher's preference, the discussion questions can be used during the warm up, wrap up, or as a supplement if the activity runs short.

Set up

Tell students a politician has invited two researchers to his or her office. The politician is unfamiliar with human cloning and wants more information. The researchers will try to convince the politician that their opinion is the correct one.

Hand each student in the group a role play card and give them time to read it. If you have a group of four, give two students politician cards. Tell students they shouldn't show their group members their card, but the politician should identify themselves.

Explain any unfamiliar vocabulary from the cards, i.e., treatment options, organs, leap, informed decision, etc. Give students time to think of arguments for their role. You may want to give them additional time to do

research on their phones to learn more about the arguments for and against their position.

Role play

Students should arrange their desks so the two researchers are facing the politician. Tell students they shouldn't just read their cards out loud. They should make their own sentences. If you have a problem with this, just tell them to put the cards away or collect them.

All groups in the class will do the role play at the same time while the teacher monitors and makes notes of common errors. Try not to interrupt or interfere with the role play unless absolutely necessary.

Give students around seven minutes to complete the role play. The role play may run short or long depending on how outgoing and confident your students are.

When one or two groups look like they are winding down, let the other groups know they have one minute to finish up.

Wrap up

Elicit from each politician whether they are now for or against human cloning.

Discussion Questions

- Do you know how scientists clone animals? What is the process?

- Do you think scientists should be allowed to clone people?

- Would you want to have a clone of yourself?

- What problems could cloning people solve?

- Could cloning people lead to problems? What kinds of problems?

- If we could clone dinosaurs like in Jurassic Park, would you want to?

- How about if we could clone ancient humans, like Neanderthals or the early Homo sapiens? Would you want to clone ancient humans?

- What if science could clone famous people like Albert Einstein or Leonardo Da Vinci? Do you think they would be as successful if they were brought back as clones?

- How can cloning animals help science?

- What do you think cloning will be like in the future? Will cloning stop or expand?

CLONING

Role Play Cards

Role 1
For cloning

You must convince the politician that human cloning is a good idea.

If human cloning becomes legal, it will cause a huge leap forward in research. Scientists will be able to learn much more about the human body and the diseases that affect it. There will be diseases that are cured and many more treatment options. Researchers could clone individual organs for people and keep them in storage until the person needs them. A full human wouldn't need to be cloned, just the organs. Human cloning would also allow parents who aren't able to have children to raise a child who is a clone of one of the parents.

Role 2
Against cloning

You must convince the politician that human cloning should not be done.

If human cloning becomes legal, it will be a disaster. People will clone themselves and keep their clones locked away until their organs are needed. Clones might not be treated like people. There will also be lots of clones of celebrities and famous people. Lots of people will want a clone of their favorite celebrity instead of having children the natural way. Another concern is that we don't know what medical side effects will occur if we clone humans.

Role 3
The politician

You are trying to decide if human cloning should or shouldn't be done.

You have invited two researchers into your office to discuss human cloning. You have an open mind about cloning, and you want to hear the pros and cons of human cloning to decide whether you support it or not. Listen to what the researchers have to say. Ask lots of questions. If you aren't sure about a point, ask for more detail. Make an informed decision as to whether human cloning is a good idea or a bad idea.

Color Role Play

Lesson Plan

Description – Apartment managers must decide what color to paint the exterior and interior of the apartment building.

Preparation - Copy / cut role play cards before class. Prepare one role play card per student. Prepare a picture of an apartment building (optional).

Warm up

Divide students into groups of three. A group of two can be made if necessary. Elicit some colors and write them on the board. Ask groups to discuss how each of the different colors make them feel. For each of the colors, you can ask them to imagine being in a room painted that color. Elicit some of their thoughts and point out any differences in how certain colors make people feel.

Note - The discussion questions are about color in general, not just about color use in buildings. Depending on the teacher's preference, the discussion questions can be used during the warm up, wrap up, or as a supplement if the activity runs short.

Set up

Tell students they are managers of an apartment building. If you prepared a picture of an apartment building, show your students and tell them that this is their apartment building. It's time to paint the outside and hallways of the apartment building. They must decide on a color scheme to use.

Hand each student in the group a role play card and give them time to read it. If you have a group of two, you can leave out role card three. Tell students they shouldn't show their group members their card. Explain any unfamiliar vocabulary from the cards, i.e., color scheme, interior, etc. Give students time to think of arguments for their role.

Remind them they must come to a decision by the end of the role play.

Role play

Students should arrange their desks so they are facing each other. All groups in the class will do the role play at the same time while the teacher monitors and makes notes of common errors. Try not to interrupt or interfere with the role play unless absolutely necessary.

Give students around ten minutes to complete the role play. The role play may run short or long depending on how outgoing and confident your students are.

When one or two groups have come to a decision, let the other groups know they have two minutes to finish up.

Wrap up

Elicit from each group what colors they decided to paint the apartment building.

Discussion Questions

- What is your favorite color?

- Is color important to you?

- Does color affect your emotions?

- Why do you think colors affect humans so much?

- Do you think that certain colors are only for boys or only for girls?

- Which colors do guys usually like more? How about girls? Why do you think there is a difference?

- If you HAD to change your hair color, what color would you change it to?

- Most electronics are either black, silver or white. Why do you think this is? Do you think we will have more colorful electronics in the future?

- If you bought a car, what color would it be?

- Can you think of some examples of color used as camouflage in daily life?

Role Play Cards

Role I
Bright and cheerful

You want to paint the apartment bright and cheerful colors.

You think that the outside of the apartment should be painted bright and cheerful colors to catch the attention of new residents and to let them know this is a great apartment to move to. The interior hallways should also be bright colors to cheer up the residents and keep them in a good mood. You really don't want the interior of the apartments to be a dark color. It will make people depressed and make the hallways look dirty. Your goal is to get everyone to agree to paint the exterior and interior bright cheerful colors.

Role 2
Dark and calming

You want to paint the apartment dark and calming colors.

You think that the outside and inside hallways should be painted dark calming colors like dark blues and grays. It hides dirt a lot better so the apartments will look cleaner for longer. It's also good to help residents relax and calm down when they come home. Plus, dark calming colors look a lot more professional for the outside of the apartment. You really don't want the exterior of the apartment to be a bright color. Your goal is to get everyone to agree to paint the exterior and interior a dark calming color scheme.

Role 3
Natural colors

You want to paint the apartment natural colors.

You think that the new color scheme should be based on natural colors. Lots of green, brown, tan, and gray. You think that painting the apartment natural colors will make it more inviting and comfortable for new residents and current residents. You don't really care whether the colors are dark or bright, but they should be colors from nature. You want residents to feel like they are connected to nature even though they live in an apartment. Your goal is to get everyone to agree to paint the exterior and interior with natural colors.

Cooking Role Play

Lesson Plan

Description - Chefs argue for why they should keep their job.

Preparation - Copy / cut role play cards before class. Prepare one role play card per student.

Warm up

Divide the class into groups of four. A group of three can be made if necessary. Ask groups to brainstorm some reasons why a chef might get fired. Go over their ideas as a class. Then, ask them to brainstorm what qualities a good chef has and elicit some examples.

Note - The discussion questions are about cooking in general, not just about chefs. Depending on the teacher's preference, the discussion questions can be used during the warm up, wrap up, or as a supplement if the activity runs short.

Set up

Tell groups the restaurant they work for is losing business because of complaints, and they can only keep one chef. The manager must choose which chef to keep.

Hand each student in the group a role play card and give them time to read it. Explain any unfamiliar vocabulary from the cards.

Give the manager role card to a more outgoing student if possible. If you have a group of three you can leave out a chef role card. Tell the students not to show their cards to the group. Tell the managers to identify themselves but not show their card.

Give managers time to think of questions to ask and the chef's time to plan how they will keep their job.

Groups should arrange their desks or chairs so that the chefs' desks are facing the manager like an interview. Explain that at the end of the role play the manager will make the decision of who to keep. Chefs should do anything they can to keep their job.

Role play

Students can stay seated. All groups in the class will do the role play at the same time while the teacher monitors and makes notes of common errors. Try not to interrupt or interfere with the role play unless absolutely necessary.

Give students around ten minutes to complete the role play. The role play may run short or long depending on how outgoing and confident your students are. When one or two groups look like they are finished, tell the other groups they have one minute to finish up.

Wrap up

For each group, ask the manager who they decided to keep and why.

Discussion Questions

- Would you like to be a chef? Why?

- How hard is it to become a chef? What do you have to do to become a chef?

- How often do you cook?

- If you had your own personal chef, what meal would you ask for most often?

- How good are you at cooking? What are some things that you can cook?

- What dish or food are you best at cooking?

- Do you think you can cook better than your mother?

- Who is a better cook, your mother or your grandmother?

- Are cooking shows popular in your country? Do you watch any cooking shows?

- What are some of the advantages of cooking your meals at home? How about the disadvantages?

- Is it important for husbands to know how to cook?

- Does your father cook?

- Who is the best cook you know?

Role Play Cards

Role 1
The manager

You are a manager of a restaurant. The owner of the restaurant has told you that you can only keep one chef. Your goal is to choose the best chef to keep.

There has been a lot of complaints from customers and bad online reviews. This has caused business to decline at the restaurant so now you can only keep one chef. The complaints are because of the chefs doing a bad job, but you are sure at least one of the chefs is really good. The owner is furious, and you think you will lose your job if you don't pick the right chef to keep. You can't fire all the chefs because then the restaurant will close.

Role 2
Chef one

You are a chef at a restaurant. Your goal is to keep your job.

The chefs you work with are amateurs. They are always making mistakes. You believe that if you can get rid of the other chefs you can make this restaurant amazing. If you are put in charge of the kitchen, you can turn this restaurant into the most popular restaurant in the city. You'll become a famous chef like you have dreamed of since you were a child.

Role 3
Chef two

You are a chef at a restaurant. Your goal is to keep your job.

You've been working really hard, but it's difficult to concentrate because you are a single parent with three kids. You've got a lot of stress and lots to worry about. Sometimes you make mistakes because you are too tired and stressed out. You need this job though. Your kids are depending on you. You'll do anything to keep this job. You don't know what your family will do if you lose this job.

Role 4
Chef three

You are a chef at a restaurant. Your goal is to keep your job.

You hate this restaurant, and you really hate the owner. When this restaurant opened it caused your family's restaurant to close. Your grandfather started that restaurant 50 years ago. You trained as a chef to work in your family's restaurant, but when you graduated from culinary school it closed because of this restaurant. You got a job here so you could destroy the restaurant from the inside. It's almost closed, but you have to lie to keep your job so you can finish destroying this restaurant.

Crime Role Play

Lesson Plan

Description - A police officer must decide which suspect is guilty.

Preparation - Copy / cut role play cards before class. Prepare one role play card per student.

Warm up

Divide students into groups of three. A group of four can be made if necessary. Ask students to brainstorm some techniques police officers use to get criminals to confess. Go over them as a class and write them on the board. Ask groups to discuss which techniques are the most effective.

Note - The discussion questions are about crime in general. Depending on the teacher's preference, the discussion questions can be used during the warm up, wrap up, or as a supplement if the activity runs short.

Set up

Tell students that one suspect in each group is guilty, but the police officer doesn't know who. They must ask questions to find the guilty person. At the end of the role play, the police officers will be asked who they will charge with the crime, and we'll see if they are punishing the guilty or the innocent person.

Hand each student in the group a role play card and give them time to read it. If you have a group of four you can make two of them police officers. Tell students they must not show their group members their card or tell them what is on it. Explain any unfamiliar vocabulary from the cards.

Tell students that police officers should brainstorm some questions to ask, and suspects should think of details for their story of what happened. Give students time to prepare.

Role play

Set up the desks up like an interrogation area, with the police officer facing the two suspects. All groups in the class will do the role play at the same time while the teacher monitors and makes notes of common errors. Try not to interrupt or interfere with the role play unless absolutely necessary.

Give students around eight minutes to complete the role play. The role play may run short or long depending on how outgoing and confident your students are.

Once it looks like one or two groups are winding down, tell the groups they have one minute to finish.

Wrap up

For each group, ask the police officer which suspect they think is guilty. Then, tell the guilty suspect to reveal themselves and see if the officer made the correct guess.

Discussion Questions

- What do you think the most common crime in your country is?

- Should police in your country be stricter or less strict?

- Is your country a safe country?

- Have you ever seen a crime? (Don't talk about it if it's too upsetting for you.)

- Do you think criminals can change?

- Is shoplifting common in your country? What kind of people shoplift and what kinds of things do they steal?

- What is the best way for police to keep neighborhoods safe?

- Does your country have a crime group like the mafia?

- Have you ever met someone from a mafia?

- Can you tell if a kid will grow up to be a criminal?

CRIME

Role Play Cards

Role 1
Police officer

You are a police officer. You have brought in two people who were fighting. You must determine which one is the guilty suspect.

You were driving your police car around when you saw two people fighting over a baseball bat. They both have bruises and are bleeding. They both claim the other one threatened to beat them with the baseball bat if they didn't give them money. They also both claim they fought back to defend themselves. Both of their fingerprints are on the baseball bat, and neither of them has been arrested before. Your goal is to find the guilty suspect.

Role 2
Suspect one

You were brought into a police station. You must convince the police officer you are innocent.

You tried to steal money from someone by threatening to hit them with a baseball bat, but they fought back. Before you could win the fight and take their money, a police car pulled up. You decided the best way to get away is to lie and convince the police officer that the other person threatened you with the baseball bat and tried to steal your money. Your goal is to make the police officer believe you are innocent and that the other person is guilty.

Role 3
Suspect two

You were brought into a police station. You must convince the police officer you are innocent.

You were walking down the street when someone came up and threatened to hit you with a baseball bat if you didn't give them your money, but you fought back to defend yourself. Thankfully, a police car pulled up. However, the thief lied and said he was innocent and you were trying to steal his money! The police officer brought you both to the police station. Your goal is to make the police officer believe you are innocent and the other person is guilty.

Dating Role Play

Lesson Plan

Description - Students choose a famous person to be and then speed date but keep their name a secret.

Preparation - Copy / cut a "Question Card" for each student (optional).

Warm up

Put students in pairs. Elicit / explain what speed dating is. Ask pairs to brainstorm some questions that would be good to ask while speed dating. After a while, go around the class and ask pairs for some of their ideas.

Note - The discussion questions are about dating in general. Depending on the teacher's preference, the discussion questions can be used during the warm up, wrap up, or as a supplement if the activity runs short.

Set up

Tell students they should choose a celebrity they know well, but they shouldn't tell anyone who that celebrity is.

Tell the class they will speed date, and they will be the celebrity they chose. The celebrity can be a different gender than they are. All the celebrities at the speed dating event are in disguise. Tell them their fellow classmates could be any celebrity.

While speed dating, they shouldn't tell anyone what their name is. It should be a secret. They can let other students know anything else about themselves, just not their name.

They will choose only one person for another date. Their goal will be to try to get as many people as possible to choose them for another date.

Hand out the "Question Cards" if you are using them. Give students time to come up with questions to ask.

Role play

Have the students stand facing their partner in two lines or sit at their desks facing their partner. Rotate one line of students clockwise so they are facing a new partner and know how to rotate.

The students will have three minutes to ask their speed date partner questions. After three minutes, tell the students who are rotating to rotate clockwise to the next partner. Repeat this for five turns or until students get back to their original partner. Then, rotate once more but don't let them ask any questions. (This ensures that the person they just finished talking to isn't obliged to choose them.) Ask each student to choose one person they want to go on a date with, tell why they want to go on a date with them, and ask them who they think that person is.

After all the students have finished picking who they want to go out on a date with, congratulate the two most popular people and congratulate any students who chose each other to go on a date with.

Lastly, have each student reveal which celebrity they are.

Wrap up

Put students back in their original pairs and have them discuss whether they would like to actually try speed dating and why or why not.

Discussion Questions

- Where is the best place in your city to take a date?

- What can you do if you want to save money and go on a date?

- How common are blind dates in your country?

- Do most blind dates go well? If not, why not?

- What is the best way to meet boyfriends or girlfriends?

- Describe your ideal date.

- What was the worst / best date that you have ever been on?

- When two people go on a date, who should pay?

- How many people should you date before getting married?

- What do you think of double dates?

Question Card

Questions

What questions will you ask in order to find your perfect partner?

You are a celebrity. You are going to speed date with other mystery celebrities.

Write down some questions you want to ask. Remember, you can't ask about their name, but you can ask anything else. All the other celebrities are using disguises, just like you. You shouldn't tell anyone what your name is. What do you want to know about someone before going on a date with them?

Questions

- _____

- _____

- _____

- _____

- _____

Dreaming Role Play

Lesson Plan

Description - Students go to dream analysts who tell them what their dream means.

Preparation - Make a copy of the "Dream Sheet" for each student (optional). Find an example of a dream online.

Warm up

Ask students to give you some examples of the meaning of things in dreams from their culture. *Example: Does it mean anything if you lose a tooth in a dream?* What are some good things to dream about? What are some bad things to dream about?

Put students in groups of four. Make a group of three or five if necessary. Give students the example of the dream you found online. Ask them what they think it means. Tell them to be creative in their interpretation.

Note - The discussion questions are about dreams in general, not just about dream interpretation. Depending on the teacher's preference, the discussion questions can be used during the warm up, wrap up, or as a supplement if the activity runs short.

Set up

Tell students they are going to visit dream analysts who will tell them the meaning of a dream.

Give each student in class the "Dream Sheet" if you decide to use it. Tell them to make notes about a dream they had. Tell them DON'T share a dream that is too personal or embarrassing. Emphasize this or you will have some students sharing uncomfortable details. If they can't think of a dream, they can make up one. Give students time to write notes about their dream.

Divide the class in half. Half of the students will be dream analysts and the other half will be customers. If there is an odd number of students, make two students a dream analyst team. Encourage dream analysts to be creative in their interpretations.

Role play

Have all the students stand up and set up the desks with one desk facing another. Have all the dream analysts sit facing the same way so they have an empty seat in front of them. Next, let all the customers sit down in front of a dream analyst of their choice.

1ˢᵗ Round

They will have three minutes to talk about their dream and get their analysis of it. After three minutes, tell customers to rotate clockwise to the dream analyst next to them and get a different dream interpretation for three minutes. Repeat this for four turns or until students get back to their original dream analyst.

2ⁿᵈ Round

After the 1ˢᵗ round, customers and dream analysts switch roles. Dream analysts will pull out their "Dream Sheet" (or their notes if you aren't using the "Dream Sheet") and become customers. After they switch roles, customers rotate around just like in the 1ˢᵗ round.

Wrap up

Ask students who gave them the most accurate or interesting interpretation of their dream. Optionally, you can have a poll to see who the best dream analyst was.

DREAMING

Discussion Questions

- How often do you dream?

- Do you dream in color or black and white?

- Have you ever had a flying dream?

- Have you ever been falling in a dream and, just when you are about to hit the ground, you wake up?

- Do you think dreams have meanings?

- Do you think dreams can tell the future?

- Have you ever been dreaming and woken up and couldn't move?

- What was the best or worst dream you can remember? Don't share your dream if it's too personal or too intense.

- Why do we forget dreams so quickly?

- Have you ever kept a dream journal?

- Why do we dream? What is the purpose of them?

- Do you think animals dream, too? What kind of dreams do you think they have?

- What does your country's culture traditionally believe about dreams?

- Have you ever had déjà vue?

Dream Sheet

Dream

Visiting a dream analyst

You are going to a dream analyst who will tell you what your dream means.

Remember, don't talk about a dream that is too personal or potentially embarrassing. If you can't think of a dream, you can make one up.

Brief summary or notes about the dream:

_____

_____

_____

_____

_____

_____

_____

Confusing parts of the dream:

- _____

- _____

- _____

Most vivid parts of the dream:

- _____

- _____

- _____

Entrepreneurs Role Play

Lesson Plan

Description - Students create a business idea and try to get funding for their idea.

Preparation - Make a copy of the "Startup Sheet" for each pair (optional).

Warm up

Put students into pairs. If there is an odd number, make a group of three. Elicit / teach students what an entrepreneur is. Ask the pairs to brainstorm names of some entrepreneurs and the companies they started. Elicit some of their ideas. Most will be famous entrepreneurs but remind students that most entrepreneurs start small to medium sized businesses.

Note - The discussion questions are about entrepreneurs in general, not just about funding for startups. Depending on the teacher's preference, the discussion questions can be used during the warm up, wrap up, or as a supplement if the activity runs short.

Set up

Tell pairs they will create a startup together. Remind students that the most important thing for a business to have is a problem to solve. Have pairs brainstorm some problems in their own lives and businesses and solutions that might resolve those problems.

When it looks like most pairs have some ideas, give each pair in class the "Startup Sheet" if you decide to use it. Tell them they are going to try to get funding for their startup. Pairs will fill out the sheet and / or make notes. Tell them to also think about what questions the investors might ask.

When most of the pairs look like they are finished, split each pair. One student will be an investor, and one will try to get money for the startup.

Role play

Have the students set up the desks with two desks facing each other. Have all the investors sit facing the same way so they are facing their partner who will be the entrepreneur trying to get money for their startup. Remind investors they have the power to destroy or make the entrepreneurs' dreams come true. They will choose only one business to invest in. Entrepreneurs rotate clockwise so they are facing an investor who is not their partner.

1st Round

Entrepreneurs will have two minutes to pitch their business idea to the investor. After two minutes, tell entrepreneurs to rotate clockwise to the investor next to them and pitch their idea again for two minutes. Repeat this for four turns or until students get back to their original partner. Have the entrepreneurs stand up at the front of the class and ask the investors which business they will chose. Congratulate the business with the most investors.

2nd Round

After the 1st round, pairs discuss what the entrepreneur learned. Entrepreneurs and investors then switch roles. Repeat the instructions for the 1st round going counter clockwise this time.

Wrap up

After the role play is finished, ask the winners of each round about their businesses, and ask the class what they thought the most effective strategies for getting funding were.

Discussion Questions

- What are four pros and four cons of being an entrepreneur?

- Do you know any entrepreneurs?

- Does your country have a lot of entrepreneurs? Why do you think so?

- What is the most profitable type of business to open in your country?

- Should a restaurant open where there are no restaurants or lots of restaurants?

- In your country, is it better for a restaurant or café to be unique or to be familiar?

- How are businesses today different from businesses in the past?

- What must a company do or have to be successful?

- Are people born entrepreneurs or are they made?

- What traits make someone a good entrepreneur?

- Would you like to open your own business? Why or why not?

Startup Sheet

> ### Startup
> *The next big thing!*

You are going to create a startup and try to get funding for it.

Be creative but remember to be practical. Investors want a good return on their money, but they also want to invest in businesses that are realistic. Don't make your business too big or too small.

Name of startup:

What is the problem your start up solves?

_____

_____

_____

How does your startup solve the problem?

_____

_____

_____

How is your startup different from other similar businesses?

_____

_____

_____

How much money do you need?

_____

_____

_____

Who are your customers and how big is the market?

_____

_____

_____

Environmental Problems Role Play

Lesson Plan

Description - A government is trying to decide how to use a large lake near a national park. Different interest groups are lobbying to use the lake.

Preparation - Copy / cut role play cards before class. Prepare one role play card per student.

Warm up

Divide the class into groups of four. A group of three can be made if necessary. Write these questions on the board: "What are some local environmental problems you know about?" "Is preserving the local environment more, or less, important than improving the local economy? Why?" Let students discuss and then elicit some ideas after they have finished.

Note - The discussion questions focus more on global environmental problems whereas the role play focuses on local environmental problems. Depending on the teacher's preference, the discussion questions can be used during the warm up, wrap up, or as a supplement if the activity runs short.

Set up

Tell groups the government is trying to decide what to do with a large lake that is next to a national forest. Several advocates have a plan for the lake and a government official must choose what to use the lake for.

Hand each student in the group a role play card and give them time to read it. If you have a group of three, you can take out role card two. Tell students they shouldn't show their group members their card. Explain any unfamiliar vocabulary from the cards.

Give the advocates time to prepare their arguments and the government official time to think of questions.

Explain that at the end of the role play the government official will choose only one of the advocates' plans. Advocates should tear down the other advocates arguments and convince the official to choose their plan.

Role play

Students can stay seated or do their role play standing up with the official sitting down. All groups in the class will do the role play at the same time while the teacher monitors and makes notes of common errors. Try not to interrupt or interfere with the role play unless absolutely necessary.

Give students around ten minutes to complete the role play. The role play may run short or long depending on how outgoing and confident your students are.

Once it looks like one or two of the groups are finishing up, give the other groups one or two minutes to finish up their role plays.

Wrap up

Ask each government official their decision and why they chose the plan they did.

Discussion Questions

- What are some of the most serious environmental problems?

- What are ten things individuals can do to help the environment?

- What are five things governments can do to help the environment?

- What is your opinion on climate change?

- Which countries cause the most pollution?

- How will our children be affected by climate change?

- What kinds of technologies do you know of that might help stop environmental problems?

- Are corporations responsible for helping the environment?

- What are some things that corporations can do to help the environment?

- What are some local environmental problems you have noticed?

- Do you think houses will be more environmentally friendly in the future?

- Where will we get our energy when we run out of oil?

- How will India and China affect the environment in the future?

- What will happen if we keep polluting the environment?

- Will the climate keep changing or go back to normal?

ENVIRONMENTAL PROBLEMS

Role Play Cards

Role 1
The nuclear power plant advocate

You work for a company that builds nuclear power plants. You must convince a government official to let your company build a nuclear power plant near the lake.

Building a nuclear power plant would mean more jobs and cheaper electricity for nearby cities. The lake is a good distance from any residents, so no one will complain about radiation if we build it near the lake. The nuclear power plant will use and pollute the water from the lake, but nuclear power means there is no air pollution, like with other power plants. Even though this lake would be polluted, it would help the environment more than it would hurt it.

Role 2
The local tourism advocate

You are part of the local tourism board. You must convince a government official to let hotel companies build resorts on the lake.

If hotel companies are allowed to build resorts around the lake, the resorts will bring in more tax revenue from the companies. The tourists will also bring in more money for local businesses. The lake might get some pollution from the resorts, but the pollution won't be as bad as a nuclear power plant. If a nuclear power plant is put by the lake, the lake won't be able to be used as a tourism destination.

Role 3
The environmental advocate

You are part of a local environmental NGO. You must convince a government official to make the lake part of the neighboring national forest.

The lake is already next the national forest. It would be easy for the government to simply add it to the national forest. Adding a lake to the national forest would give animals a safe source of water and increase the population of the local wildlife and improve the local ecosystem. If a nuclear power plant or a bunch of resorts are built, the lake won't be able to be used by the local wildlife. The lake will be polluted by the nuclear power plant or the waste from the resorts. Also, if the lake is left untouched it can be a safe place for local residents to take their families.

Role 4
The government official

You will decide how a large lake will be used. Listen to the advocates' arguments and decide the best use of the lake.

You are in charge of land development for the area. Your main goal is to do what is best for the local residents and the surrounding areas. You must choose only one of the plans the advocates bring you. Remember, you have the power in the situation, so don't be afraid to challenge the advocates and ask tough questions.

Ethics Role Play

Lesson Plan

Description - Government officials must decide how to handle the outbreak of a terrible new disease.

Preparation - Copy / cut role play cards before class. Prepare one role play card per student. Research the trolley problem and fat man variation if you aren't already aware of them (optional). Simply Google "trolley problem" to find out more.

Warm up

Divide students into groups of three. A group of two can be made if necessary. Write this sentence on the board: "Is it ethical to kill a few people to save many people?" Have groups discuss and elicit some of their thoughts.

Optionally, the teacher can give the students the trolley problem along with the fat man variation. More details can be found by Googling "trolley problem".

Note - The discussion questions are about ethics and ethical behavior in general. Depending on the teacher's preference, the discussion questions can be used during the warm up, wrap up, or as a supplement if the activity runs short.

Set up

Tell students there is a new mysterious disease spreading quickly through a city killing thousands of people. The disease doesn't seem to have spread outside of the city, but health officials don't know for certain if it has or hasn't. Tell students they are the government officials who must decide what to do about the situation.

Hand each student in the group a role play card and give them time to read it. If you have a group of two, you can leave out role card

two. Tell students they shouldn't show their group members their card. Explain any unfamiliar vocabulary from the cards (quarantine, lethal / non-lethal force, etc.). Give students time to think of arguments based on their card.

Remind them they must come to a decision by the end of the role play.

Role play

Students should arrange their desks so they are facing each other. All groups in the class will do the role play at the same time while the teacher monitors and makes notes of common errors. Try not to interrupt or interfere with the role play unless absolutely necessary.

Give students around ten minutes to complete the role play. The role play may run short or long depending on how outgoing and confident your students are.

When one or two groups have come to a decision, let the other groups know they have two minutes to finish up.

Wrap up

Elicit from each group what they decided to do with the city and why.

Discussion Questions

- Do you consider yourself to be an ethical person?

- Have you ever found a smart phone? What did you do? If you haven't, what do you think you would do?

- Would you risk your life to save another person?

- Would you jump into a deep river to save a drowning animal?

- What should a person do if they find a wallet? What do people usually do? What would you do?

- What are some ethical dilemmas you have faced?

- Is stealing ALWAYS wrong? When is it right to steal?

- How often do you lie? When is it okay to lie?

- What makes a person act ethically or unethically?

- If you saw a pickpocket stealing someone's wallet what would you do?

- Should poor people be punished for stealing if they are stealing to feed their family?

ETHICS

Role Play Cards

Role 1
Stop the disease by any means necessary.

You believe the right thing to do is to quarantine the city. Block all roads, and, with lethal force, stop everyone from leaving.

If anyone is allowed to leave the city it raises the chance that this new infectious disease will spread to lots of other cities. It's better to be firm and stop the disease here before it spreads and kills many more people. It would be much better to kill everyone in this city, healthy or unhealthy, than risk it spreading to other cities. Your goal is to bomb the city and kill everyone in the city to stop the spread. If no one will agree, you at least want to kill anyone who tries to leave the city.

Role 2
Stop the disease but try to not kill anyone.

You believe the right thing to do is to quarantine the city. Block all roads, and try to stop everyone from leaving, without using lethal force.

If anyone is allowed to leave the city it raises the chance that this new infectious disease will spread to lots of other cities. You want to stop as many people as you can from leaving, but you don't feel it's ethical to kill anyone who is trying to escape the city. Your goal is to use tear gas, rubber bullets, and other means to stop people from leaving the city. Even if some sick people escape, it's better than killing innocent healthy people.

Role 3
Try to save the people in the city.

You believe the right thing to do is not to quarantine the city but to try to help the people in the city.

If the city is quarantined it will stop people from going in and helping the sick and protecting the healthy. If the roads are blocked off, it means that lots of sick people might die unnecessarily, and it means that all the healthy people who are trapped in the city with the sick people will probably die, too. Your goal is to let the healthy people leave the city or stay in their homes and have health care professionals go in to help the sick. The disease could have already spread, so even if everyone in the city was killed it might not make a difference.

Family Role Play

Lesson Plan

Description - A family argues over who should do which chores.

Preparation - Copy / cut role play cards before class. Prepare one role play card per student. Make a copy of the "Chores Sheet" for each group (optional).

Warm up

Divide the class into groups of three. A group of two can be made if necessary. Ask groups to brainstorm five household chores and rank them in order of how much they hate them. So, first on the list would be the worst chore. Have groups write them on the board in order.

Note - The discussion questions are about family / families in general, not just about family fights. Depending on the teacher's preference, the discussion questions can be used during the warm up, wrap up, or as a supplement if the activity runs short.

Set up

Give groups the "Chores Sheet" and tell them to add three more.

After they are finished adding the chores, tell the groups that they are a family. There is only one parent because of a divorce, and there are two children. They must decide who will do which chores.

Hand each student in the group a role play card and give them time to read it.

Note - If you have a group of two you can leave out role card one and explain that the siblings will have to decide who does what by themselves.

Tell the students not to show their cards to the group. Tell the parents to identify themselves but not show their cards. Explain any unfamiliar vocabulary from the cards.

Role play

Students should stay seated and move their chairs so it's like a family sitting around a table. All groups in the class will do the role play at the same time while the teacher monitors and makes notes of common errors. Try not to interrupt or interfere with the role play unless absolutely necessary.

Give students around ten minutes to complete the role play. The role play may run short or long depending on how outgoing and confident your students are. When one or two groups look like they are finished, tell groups they have two minutes to decide who does which chores.

Wrap up

Each group should tell the class how they split up the chores and why.

Discussion Questions

- Who did / does most of the chores in your family? Why?

- How did you decide who did / does most of the chores in your family?

- How do members of a family support each other?

- Who do you think has the most power in the family? Why?

- How close are you to your extended family? (cousins, aunts, etc.)

- What is the perfect number of children a family should have?

- What do you think of people who marry and decide not to have children?

- What do you think is the most important thing to make a happy family?

- Is it better for mothers to stay at home with kids or go to work to earn more money for the family?

- Many families send their children to private institutes or daycares for most of the day. Is this good or bad?

- How do you think family life is changing in your country? (Example: wife working, husband cleaning, kids at institutes) Is this change good or bad?

- What do you think of gay marriage?

- Is spanking or hitting a good way to discipline children? Why or why not?

- What age is too young to get married?

Chores Sheet

- Take out the trash

- Do the dishes

- Cook

- Clean the bathroom (once a week)

- Do the laundry

-

-

-

Role Play Cards

Role 1
The Parent

You are the only parent. You have a job and you are tired of doing all the housework. Your goal is to split up the chores between your two children.

You are exhausted from working and trying to raise two children. They are old enough to be doing chores so they should help out around the house. You think your children might be becoming spoiled and lazy. You think that doing more work will help them mature and be better adults when they grow up.

Role 2
The Older Child

You are the older child. Your goal is to agree to do as few chores as possible.

Your parent is trying to get you to do chores but you want to try and avoid doing them. Tell your family that you have to go to soccer practice every day so you can't do chores. But secretly you only have practice every other day. You want more time to hang out with your friends. Your sibling says they have to study but you've seen them playing on their phone when they say they are studying. **You refuse to: clean the bathroom, cook, or do the dishes.**

Role 3
The Younger Child

You are the younger child. Your goal is to agree to do as few chores as possible.

Your parent is trying to get you to do chores but you want to try and avoid doing them. Tell your family that you have to study hard every day to get better grades, so you can't do chores. But secretly you want more time to play games on your phone in your room. Your sibling says they have to go to soccer practice every day but you think they are hanging out with their friends instead of practicing soccer. **You refuse to: take out the trash, cook, or clean the bathroom.**

Fast Food Role Play

Lesson Plan

Description – Politicians debate whether or not to tax / ban fast food.

Preparation - Copy / cut role play cards before class. Prepare one role play card per student.

Warm up

Divide students into groups of three. A group of two can be made if necessary. Ask groups to come up with a definition of what fast food is and some examples of typical fast food. Ask students to brainstorm some of the good and bad things about fast food. Have them write their ideas on the board in two columns.

Note – The discussion questions are about fast food in general rather than government regulation of fast food. Depending on the teacher's preference, the discussion questions can be used during the warm up, wrap up, or as a supplement if the activity runs short.

Set up

A new law about fast food is being debated. The government has to pay a lot of money towards health care for obesity related diseases. The new law would put a tax on unhealthy fast food, which would raise the prices of unhealthy fast food. The tax would be applied based on the weight of the food vs. calories / fat / sugar. A fast food restaurant will be a restaurant where people can get their food to go. The law won't apply to regular restaurants.

The money from the tax would go towards paying for health care costs of obesity related diseases. Some of the money would go into ad campaigns that help fight obesity.

The students are politicians deciding how they will vote on the new law. They can choose to vote no, yes, or to amend the law. They will try to convince their fellow politicians to vote their way.

Hand each student in the group a role play card and give them time to read it. If you have a group of two, you can leave out role card three. Tell students they shouldn't show their group members their card. Explain any unfamiliar vocabulary from the cards, i.e., ban, obesity, amend, etc. Give students time to think of arguments to support their role.

Role play

Students can stay seated in a group or do their role play standing up.

All groups in the class will do the role play at the same time while the teacher monitors and makes notes of common errors. Try not to interrupt or interfere with the role play unless absolutely necessary.

Give students around seven minutes to complete the role play. The role play may run short or long depending on how outgoing and confident your students are.

When one or two groups seem to have stopped debating, tell the rest of the groups they have one minute to come to a decision about what to do.

Wrap up

Ask each individual student how they will vote and tally the votes up for the class to see if the law will be struck down, implemented, or amended.

Discussion Questions

- What is your least favorite fast food restaurant and why? How about your favorite fast food restaurant?

- Does fast food taste good or bad? Why?

- Why is fast food so popular?

- How often do you eat fast food? What do you usually eat? Where?

- What is a food that people think is healthy but really isn't?

- Do you know anyone who has worked at a fast food restaurant? How did they like it?

- How has fast food changed in your country?

- How is your country's fast food different from other countries' fast food?

- Can you think of any healthy fast food?

- How do you think fast food will change in the future?

Role Play Cards

Role 1

Freedom

You think everyone should vote no on the new law. The government shouldn't try to control what people eat.

People have a right to choose what they want to eat. If they want to eat cheap unhealthy food, they are free to do that. The government shouldn't interfere with what people eat by taxing it and making the food more expensive. It's very dangerous to start regulating what people do in their daily lives. It will only lead to more regulation. What's next? If people don't exercise, they have to pay a fine? Your goal is to convince your fellow politicians to vote no on the new law.

Role 2

Money

You think everyone should vote yes on the new law. The government needs to make back the money it spends on obesity related health care.

Taxing fast food would be a big win for everyone. The price of the unhealthy fast food would go up, so people would eat less and be healthier. The fast food restaurants would start offering healthier food to avoid the tax. Plus, the tax money the new law will bring in will help pay for the health care costs that the government is already paying, which means the government can lower taxes in other areas. Your goal is to convince your fellow politicians to vote yes for the new law.

Role 3

Health

You think the law doesn't go far enough. You want to amend the law to ban the sale of unhealthy food to children.

Many children are suffering from obesity related diseases. This means that as they grow older, they will grow into unhealthy adults, costing the government lots of money. Taxing fast food isn't enough. We need to ban stores and fast food restaurants from selling unhealthy fast food to children. We don't allow stores to sell alcohol or cigarettes to children, why do we let them sell fast food that is equally as unhealthy? Your goal is to convince your fellow politicians to vote to amend the law to ban the sale of unhealthy food to children.

First Impressions Role Play

Lesson Plan

Description - Students meet and greet their classmates' imaginary personas then choose who gave the best first impression. *(Note to teacher - This activity works best with eight or more students, but if you have a small class, students can use their real identities and not choose the most popular person.)*

Preparation - Make a copy of the "Identity Sheet" for each student (optional).

Warm up

Put students in pairs or groups of three. Write this question on the board: "How does a person make a good first impression?" Have the students brainstorm some ideas and then ask each group for some of their ideas.

Ask groups to brainstorm topics people talk about when they first meet, i.e., name, job, sports, etc. Then, elicit ideas. Write students' ideas on the board. Ask them to brainstorm what types of questions people ask about each topic. Encourage them to come up with more than one question for each topic. They can write them down or just discuss them, depending on the teacher's preference.

Note - Depending on the teacher's preference, the discussion questions can be used during the warm up, wrap up, or as a supplement.

Set up

Choose an outgoing student and ask their name. When they tell you their name, say, "No. Your name is [make up some ridiculous name]!" Then, ask the class what the student's new job is. Encourage outrageous ideas. Go through some of the topics on the board and elicit ideas for the student's new persona.

Now tell students they will create a new persona for themselves. Hand out the "Identity Sheet" or have students make notes about their identity on a scrap piece of paper. Give students time to brainstorm their new persona based on the topics on the board. When they

are finished, divide the class into two lines facing each other. One line will be trying to make a good impression, and the other line will be judging who made the best impression. If there is an odd number of students, make two students be a team.

Role play

Rotate the students clockwise once so they know how they will be rotating.

1st Round

The students trying to make a good impression will have two minutes to make a good impression. Encourage lying and creativity when making a good first impression. After two minutes, tell the students trying to make a good impression to rotate to the next person. Repeat this for four turns or until students get back to their original partner. Then, rotate once more but don't give them time to talk. (This ensures that the person they just finished talking to isn't obliged to choose them). Ask each student judging first impressions who they thought made the best first impression and why. Then, announce the most popular person with the most votes.

2nd Round

For the 2nd round, the people who were trying make a good first impression will now be the people judging first impressions. After switching roles, repeat the instructions from the 1st round. Try to switch rotation direction so students talk to new people.

Discussion Questions

- When you look at someone, what makes you think they are...?

    - Dangerous, greedy, intelligent, kind, not smart, crazy, generous, etc.

- Do you like to meet new people or do you prefer to hang out with people you already know?

- When and where did you meet most of your friends for the first time?

- Have you met someone who you hated right away even though you didn't know them?

- When are the most important times to make a good first impression?

- Do you make first impressions based on what people wear?

- What kind of impression are you trying to make with your clothes?

- Do you try to make a different first impression now than you did in high school?

- Have you ever tried to make a great first impression but completely messed it up?

- In what jobs do people have to make very quick decisions based on first impressions?

Identity Sheet

New Identity

Making a good first impression

You are going to create a totally new identity and try to make lots of good first impressions.

Remember, create a completely different identity. Be creative and use your imagination. Other students will judge who made the best first impression. You goal is to get the most votes. Feel free to lie!

Basic info:

- Name: _____

- Age: _____

- Job: _____

- Country: _____

More information:

_____

_____

_____

_____

_____

_____

_____

_____

_____

_____

Friendship Role Play

Lesson Plan

Description - A friend must choose between an old friend and a new friend.

Preparation - Copy / cut role play cards before class. Prepare one role play card per student.

Warm up

Divide the class into groups of three. A group of two can be made if necessary. Give students the friendship discussion questions and have them discuss whichever questions they find interesting.

Note - The discussion questions are about friendship / friends in general. Depending on the teacher's preference, the discussion questions can be used during the warm up, wrap up, or as a supplement if the activity runs short.

Set up

Hand each student in the group a role play card and give them time to read it. If you have a group of two, you can leave out role card three.

You should try to give more confident and outgoing students role card one, if possible.

Tell students they shouldn't show their group members their card, but the role one student should let the group know that they have role one. Explain any unfamiliar vocabulary from the cards.

Give students time to think of points to discuss, based on their card.

Role play

Students can stay seated, but it might be more natural if they do their role play standing up. All groups in the class will do the role play at the same time while the teacher monitors and makes notes of common errors. Try not to interrupt or interfere with the role play unless absolutely necessary.

Give students around ten minutes to complete the role play. The role play may run short or long depending on how outgoing and confident your students are. When one or two groups look like have come to a decision, give the rest of the groups two minutes to come to a decision.

Wrap up

Ask each group what their final decision was and why they made that decision.

Discussion Questions

- Do you prefer to have many friends or just a few that you are close to?

- What are the benefits of having just a few close friends? How about the benefits of having many friends?

- Describe your best friend.

- Are you close friends with anyone you knew in elementary school?

- Why do people need friends? What can happen if a person has no friends?

- How can friends be bad for a person?

- What is the biggest thing you have done to help a friend?

- Do you have any friends who would risk their life to save you?

- Would you risk your life to save a friend? How about a stranger?

- What kind of qualities do you look for in a friend?

- What is the best way to make new friends? Do you like making new friends?

- Do you think sites like Facebook are good for friendships or do they stop people from becoming close?

- How did you meet your best friend?

FRIENDSHIP

Role Play Cards

Role 1

The popular friend

You have two friends who are angry with each other.

You have two friends that are fighting over you. You really like your new friend and your old friend, but they don't get along. Your new friend tries to help you become the person you want to be. You have known your old friend since you were a child, and your old friend knows you better than anyone else. You want them both to be friends so you can all hang out together. **Your goal is to keep both friends.**

Role 2

The new friend

You have a new friend who is being held back by one of their old friends. The old friend is a bad influence, and you really don't like them.

Your new friend (role one) is great. You can imagine becoming best friends, but they have an old friend who is always hanging around and causing trouble. The old friend is rude, only talks about the past, and is always trying to get your new friend to do stupid things that will make your new friend's life worse. **Your goal is to get your new friend to stop hanging out with his old friend.**

Role 3

The old friend

You have an old friend who made a mean new friend. The new friend is trying to destroy your friendship.

Your good friend (role one) has been hanging out with a new friend. The new friend is always trying to stop you and your old friend from hanging out. When the three of you hang out, the new friend is rude and doesn't want to do anything fun. You've known your friend since you were a child, and you know them better than anyone. **Your goal is to get your old friend to stop hanging out with the new friend.**

Games / Gaming Role Play

Lesson Plan

Description - Students create an idea for a game and try to get it accepted by the board of directors of a game company.

Preparation - Make a copy of the "Game Idea Sheet" for each student (optional).

Warm up

Put students in pairs or groups of three or four. Ask them to brainstorm some of the most popular games out now for phones and tablets, PC's, and consoles. Elicit the games and write them on the board. Next, ask students to pick one or two games and talk about why they are popular. Elicit some of their ideas as to why the games are so popular.

Note — The discussion questions are based on games in general as well as video games specifically. Depending on the teacher's preference, the discussion questions can be used during the warm up, wrap up, or as a supplement.

Set up

Tell students they work for a game developer. Their company makes apps, console games, and PC games. The company needs a new breakthrough game, so the board of directors has asked every employee to come up with a game idea. If an employee's idea is chosen by one of the board members, the employee will receive a bonus. If it gets chosen by the majority of the board members, they will receive a HUGE bonus, and the game will be made. The students have to pitch their idea to board members and try to get as many board members as they can to get behind their idea.

Give them the "Game Idea Sheet" if you are using it. Otherwise, let them use their own paper to write notes.

When they are finished with their game idea or after ten minutes, divide the class into two

lines facing each other with the board members (sitting) on one side and the employees (standing) on the other side. If there is an odd number of students, make two students be a team.

Role play

Rotate the students once so they know how they will be rotating i.e., each employee moves to their right with the last one in line going to the front. Let the board members know they will choose only one game to make.

1ˢᵗ Round

The employees will have three minutes to convince the board members to make their game. After three minutes, tell the employees to rotate to the next board member. Repeat this for four turns or until students get back to their original partner. Then, rotate once more but don't let them pitch their idea. (This ensures that the person they just finished talking to isn't obliged to choose them.) Ask board members which game idea they chose. Congratulate the employee with the most votes.

2ⁿᵈ Round

For the 2ⁿᵈ round, the employees will now be the board members. After switching roles, repeat the instructions from the 1ˢᵗ round.

Wrap up

Put students back in their original groups and have them discuss which games they would most like to play.

Discussion Questions

- How many genres of video games can you name?

- How are some of these genres unique and different from the others?

- What are some of the pros and cons of the different platforms for video games?

- What are some examples of fun board games?

- Do you, or anyone you know, play card games? Which card games?

- What were some games that were popular in the past?

- What makes a good game?

- Are games good for you or bad for you?

- Are games in the present better or worse than games in the past?

- Games have been around for all of human history. Why are humans so fascinated by games?

Game Idea Sheet

Game Idea

Create a new app, PC, or console game

You get a big bonus if members of the board of directors choose to make your game. Create a game you think will be popular.

You can be creative and make a totally new and unique game, or you can use an already successful game for inspiration. Remember though, you cannot make an exact copy of an existing game.

Describe your game in one sentence:

_____

_____

_____

Game information:

- Genre: _____

- Platform(s): _____

More details about your game:

_____

_____

_____

_____

_____

_____

Why it will be popular:

_____

_____

_____

Habits Role Play

Lesson Plan

Description - Friends try to get each other to quit their bad habits.

Preparation - Copy / cut role play cards before class. Prepare one role play card per student.

Warm up

Divide students into groups of three. A group of four can be made if necessary. Ask students to brainstorm as many bad habits as they can in two minutes. It can be made into a competition by comparing the number of bad habits each group came up with and congratulating the group with the most. Elicit some of the bad habits that each group came up with.

Note - The discussion questions focus on habits in general rather than exclusively focusing on bad habits. Depending on the teacher's preference, the discussion questions can be used during the warm up, wrap up, or as a supplement if the activity runs short.

Set up

Let students know they are going to do a role play of friends having a discussion about their habits.

Hand each student in the group a role play card and give them time to read it. If you have a group of four you can make an extra copy of card four. Just let them know that instead of one of their friends having that specific bad habit, there will be two.

Tell students they shouldn't show their group members their card, but they should let their group know which habit they have. Explain any unfamiliar vocabulary from the cards. Give students time to think of arguments to support their role.

Role play

Students can stay seated in a group or do their role play standing up.

All groups in the class will do the role play at the same time while the teacher monitors and makes notes of common errors. Try not to interrupt or interfere with the role play unless absolutely necessary.

Give students around ten minutes to complete the role play. The role play may run short or long depending on how outgoing and confident your students are.

When one or two groups look like they are finished, give the rest of the groups one or two minutes to finish.

Wrap up

Ask each group who was convinced to change their habits.

Discussion Questions

- What are some things you do every day?

- What are some good habits you have?

- Do you have any bad habits?

- Can your group give you any advice for your bad habits?

- What is something you should do every day but don't?

- What are some activities you like to do?

- How much do you exercise every week?

- What is a successful life? What habits should you have in order to have a successful life?

- What three habits will improve your life?

- What are some habits that can improve your English ability?

- What is something you do about once a week, month, or year?

Role Play Cards

Role 1

The gamer

You are trying to help your friends quit their bad habits.

One of your friends spends all of their time just sitting and watching TV. Not doing anything. It's really unhealthy. Your other friend is always late! They were late today when all of you met. You play games. You love playing games on your PC or console. When you aren't at home you usually play games on your phone. It's your hobby and something you would never give up. Some of your best friends are the people you play with online. Your goal is to get your other friends to quit their bad habits, but you don't want to change your behavior.

Role 2

The TV fanatic

You are trying to help your friends quit their bad habits.

One of your friends spends all of their time playing games. It's unproductive and wastes time. You feel like your friend is wasting their life. Your other friend is late every time you all meet. It's really getting annoying. You love watching TV. It's really entertaining and gives you something to talk about with other people. It's also how you relieve stress. You can't imagine cutting back on watching TV and missing your favorite shows. Your goal is to get your other friends to quit their bad habits, but you don't want to change your behavior.

Role 3

The late one

You are trying to help your friends quit their bad habits.

Both of your friends are wasting their lives. One of them just sits and plays games; the other one just sits and watches TV. That is how they spend most of their time. You think they aren't living life to the fullest. They need to get out and experience the world. Sometimes you are late, but you live a really active lifestyle. You are always busy, so people can't really expect you to be on time all of the time. Besides, you are only sometimes late, and when you are late, it's only five or ten minutes. It's not a big deal. Your goal is to get your other friends to quit their bad habits, but you don't want to change your behavior.

Having Children Role Play

Lesson Plan

Description - In an overpopulated future, government officials must make a test for couples to pass in order to be allowed to have a child.

Preparation - Copy one "Parental Requirements Sheet" for each group (optional).

Warm up

Divide students into groups of four. A group of three can be made if necessary. Ask groups to brainstorm what some factors are that make a child turn into a successful adult. Elicit some of their ideas. Then, ask groups to discuss how much of an effect parents have on what kind of adult their child grows into.

Note - The discussion questions are about having children in general, not tests for parents. Depending on the teacher's preference, the discussion questions can be used during the warm up, wrap up, or as a supplement if the activity runs short.

Set up

Tell groups that it's 100 years in the future. The world is over populated. There will be a new law that everyone will be temporarily sterilized. *Teach "sterilized" if students are unfamiliar with it.* Couples will need to pass a test if they want to have permission to be unsterilized and have a child.

Tell groups they are on the test creation committee, and it's their job to create an outline of the test that the government will use to decide if couples will be allowed to have a child.

Tell groups they don't need to make specific questions, just a general explanation or outline of what the test will be. The test can be multiple parts and can include anything. For example, a test might have a lottery component, physical component, knowledge component, and an intelligence component.

Hand each group a "Parental Requirements Sheet" if you are using it. Tell students they must make sure that everyone on the committee is happy with the requirements for parenthood.

Role play

All groups in the class will do the role play at the same time while the teacher monitors and makes notes of common errors. Try not to interrupt or interfere with the role play unless absolutely necessary.

Give students around ten minutes to complete the role play. The role play may run short or long depending on how outgoing and confident your students are.

When one or two groups have finished their parental requirements list, let the other groups know they have one or two minutes to finish up.

Wrap up

Students present their ideas for their parental requirements.

Ask groups to discuss if it is ethically right to deny certain people the right to have children. Does it actually lead to a greater good or is it too dangerous for governments to get involved with selecting who gets to have children? You can also transition into a discussion of the dangers of eugenics, if desired.

HAVING CHILDREN

Discussion Questions

- How does having children change someone's life?

- What kinds of things do people have to give up when they have children?

- What are some of the benefits of having children?

- Do you think it is better to have children when you are older or younger?

- What is the best number of children to have? How many boys or girls?

- Do you want to have children?

    - If not - Why not? Have you told your parents about your decision? What do they think about it?

    - If so - When do you want to have children and how many do you want to have? Do you want your first child to be a boy or a girl? Why?

- Most families in wealthy countries are having less and less children. Is this a good thing or a bad thing? Why?

- How do children who have no brothers or sisters act?

- What age did women start having children sixty years ago? How about now?

Parental Requirements Sheet

Parental Test

Create the outline of a test for couples who want to have children.

Your group has been chosen by the government to make a general outline of a test that will determine the future of your country and perhaps the world. You must decide what will be on the test that will choose which couples are allowed to have children and which couples aren't. Good luck, we are all counting on you.

_____

_____

_____

_____

_____

_____

_____

_____

_____

_____

Holidays Role Play

Lesson Plan

Description - Students create a new holiday, debate which new holiday to choose and then decide how the new holiday will be implemented.

Preparation - Copy one "Create a Holiday Sheet" for each student.

Warm up

Elicit some traditional holidays and what they celebrate. Elicit some newer holidays (official or unofficial) and what they celebrate. Then, ask for ideas for a new holiday, i.e., gaming day, national exercise day, internet celebration day, etc.

Note - The discussion questions are about holidays in general. Depending on the teacher's preference, the discussion questions can be used during the warm up, wrap up, or as a supplement.

Set up

Tell students they will be creating their own holiday and trying to get it chosen by a government committee.

Give students the "Create a Holiday Sheet" and let them have around seven minutes to finish creating a new holiday.

When they are finished, divide the class into groups of three. A group of two or four can be made if necessary.

Tell the groups they are a national holiday government committee. They must choose a new holiday and decide on how it will be celebrated. Each group member has a holiday to propose to the group. After the group chooses one holiday, they will decide on any changes that need to be made, how it will be

introduced to the public, and how it will be celebrated.

Role play

Students should arrange their desks so they are facing each other. All groups in the class will do the role play at the same time while the teacher monitors and makes notes of common errors. Try not to interrupt or interfere with the role play unless absolutely necessary.

Give students around six minutes to choose the holiday and then around seven minutes to hammer out the details of the new holiday. The role play may run short or long depending on how outgoing and confident your students are.

When one or two groups have come to a decision as to what holiday to pick, let the other groups know they have two minutes to pick their holiday.

Then, allow the groups time to make changes to the holiday, decide how it will be celebrated, and how it will be implemented to the public.

Wrap up

Have each group present to the class the holiday they have chosen and their plans for celebrating the holiday.

Discussion Questions

- What is your favorite holiday? Has your favorite holiday changed since you were a kid?

- On what holiday do people in your country eat a lot of food?

- Do you give gifts on any holidays?

- What foreign holidays do you know about?

- What is the strangest holiday or festival you have heard of?

- Do you think all countries have similar holidays?

- Talk about your best memory from a holiday.

- Are there any holidays you really don't like?

- Do you think your country should have more, or less, holidays? Why?

- Does your country have parades during holidays? Have you ever been to a parade?

- What is the most important holiday?

Create a Holiday Sheet

Create a Holiday
Making a great new holiday

You are going to create a new holiday.

Remember, the holiday can celebrate anything you want, but you will need to convince your fellow committee members to choose yours, so try to make it something that will be widely popular.

Holiday info:

- Name of holiday: _____

- Date of holiday: _____

- What the holiday celebrates: _____

More details about the holiday:
(What do people do on the holiday? Do they wear anything special? Are there any special events? Etc.)

_____

_____

_____

_____

_____

_____

_____

_____

_____

_____

Homes Role Play

Lesson Plan

Description - Parents go to a housing developer to look at floor plans.

Preparation - Copy / cut role play cards before class. Prepare one role play card per student. Find an average house floor plan on Google images and make a copy for each group. Optionally, you can find more than one floor plan to give each developer.

Warm up

Divide students into groups of three. A group of two or four can be made if necessary. Try to have a mix of boys and girls in each group. Ask students to brainstorm what people look for when buying a house. Elicit some examples and write them on the board.

Note - The discussion questions are mostly about the students' homes, not homes in general. Depending on the teacher's preference, the discussion questions can be used during the warm up, wrap up, or as a supplement if the activity runs short.

Set up

Explain any unfamiliar vocabulary from the cards, i.e., developer, floor plan, commission etc.

Choose one student from each group to be a developer and hand them the floor plan and the role card. If you made more than one copy of a floor plan, give them the extra floor plans as well. If you have a group of four, make two of the students a developer team.

Tell the other two students they are a husband and wife with two kids and are looking to buy a new house. Hand each of them their role card.

Give students time to read their cards and give the mothers and fathers time to think about what they want in a house. The mother and father will each choose two things.

Role play

Students can stay seated in a group or do their role play standing up.

All groups in the class will do the role play at the same time while the teacher monitors and makes notes of common errors. Try not to interrupt or interfere with the role play unless absolutely necessary.

Give students around six minutes to complete the role play. The role play may run short or long depending on how outgoing and confident your students are.

When one or two groups look like they are winding down, tell the class they have one minute to finish up.

Wrap up

Ask each family whether they decided to buy the house or not and why.

Discussion Questions

- Is your home clean? Are you a very organized person?

- Do you have a lot of decorations in your home or is it bare?

- Are you happy with the size of your home?

- What is your favorite appliance, electronic device, or piece of furniture in your home?

- If you had $3,000 to improve your home, what would you spend it on?

- Do you agree with the saying, "Wherever I lay my head is home."?

- How is your home different from your childhood home?

- What would you say the decoration style of your home is?

- What would your ideal house or apartment look like?

- What do you do to maintain your home?

- What household chores do you hate doing?

Role Play Cards

Role 1 *Developer*

You need to sell this family a house.

If you sell this family a house, you will get a huge commission. You really need that commission. Sales haven't been good, and you're not sure if you can afford next week's bills. Show the family the floor plan, and convince them that this is the house they want. If they want something the house doesn't have, convince them they don't need what they want. You are going to have to use all of your abilities as a salesperson to make this sale.

Role 2 *Mother*

You and your husband are looking around for a house to buy in the near future.

You need a house for you, your husband, and two kids. You and your husband are just starting to shop for houses, so you don't want to buy too soon. You want to see what is out there first. You want to have an extra room you can turn into an exercise room, and you want the house to have four bathrooms. The house must also have two other things that you will decide. What two other things do you want the house to have?

Role 3 *Father*

You and your wife are looking around for a house to buy in the near future.

You need a house for you, your wife, and two kids. You and your wife are just starting to shop for houses, so you don't want to buy too soon. You want to see what is out there first. You want to have an extra room you can turn into an office, and you want the house to have a big living room for guests. The house must also have two other things that you will decide. What two other things do you want the house to have?

Hotels Role Play

Lesson Plan

Description - Hotel guests try to get their money back.

Preparation - Copy / cut role play cards before class. Prepare one role play card per hotel owner and one role play card per pair of guests.

Warm up

Divide students into groups of three. A group of two can be made if necessary. Ask groups to talk about their most memorable hotel stay. It can be a bad memory or a good memory. Elicit some stories. Then, ask students to brainstorm some things that make a hotel stay good or bad. Make two columns on the board and have them list their ideas.

Note - The discussion questions are about hotels / hostels in general. Depending on the teacher's preference, the discussion questions can be used during the warm up, wrap up, or as a supplement if the activity runs short.

Set up

Tell students that two friends stayed in a small family run hotel. The next morning the two friends go to the front desk.

Hand the most outgoing student a hotel owner card. Tell the other two they are friends and hand them the hotel guests' card.

Explain any unfamiliar vocabulary from the cards, i.e., refund, horrible, etc. Give students time to think of arguments for their role.

Tell students they must find a way to resolve the conflict so that everyone is happy.

Role play

Students should arrange the desks so the hotel owner is standing behind two desks put together like a counter and the friends are in front of the hotel owner.

All groups in the class will do the role play at the same time while the teacher monitors and makes notes of common errors. Try not to interrupt or interfere with the role play unless absolutely necessary.

Give students around six minutes to complete the role play. The role play may run short or long depending on how outgoing and confident your students are.

When one or two groups have come to a compromise, let the other groups know they have two minutes to finish up.

Wrap up

Elicit from each hotel owner what they decided to do to keep everyone happy and if they had to refund any money.

Discussion Questions

- Which do you prefer to stay in when you travel, hotels, hostels, or another type of place? Why?

- What are the best and worst things about staying in hotels?

- Have you ever been to a really disgusting hotel? Did you stay or leave?

- What do you think about people letting travelers stay at their homes instead of at hotels?

- Do you feel comfortable when you are staying at a hotel?

- Have you ever ordered room service?

- Do you have any interesting stories about staying somewhere other than your house, like a hotel or hostel?

- Are hotels common in your country? If not, where do people stay when they travel?

- What is the nicest hotel you have stayed at?

- What would it be like to work in a hotel as a cleaning person or front desk staff?

- Have you ever eaten anything out of the minibar (the refrigerator with snacks and drinks)? Was it expensive?

HOTELS

Role Play Cards

Role 1
Hotel owner

You are the owner of a small hotel and two guests are coming to complain about their room.

You have two guests that are coming to complain about their room. They stayed the whole night and didn't tell anyone about the problems they were having. If they had let you know, you could have moved them into another room, but they stayed the whole night, so you don't want to give them a refund. You think they are just trying to avoid paying for the room. Try to make them happy so they won't give you a bad review but try to avoid giving them a refund.

Role 2
Hotel guests

You and your friend are very unhappy with your hotel room, and you want your money back.

The room at the hotel was not worth the money you paid. The room had an awful smell. The beds were uncomfortable. The water in the shower was only warm and never got hot enough. The people in the room next to yours were really loud. The TV only had three channels. The air conditioner wasn't cold enough and neither was the refrigerator. It was a horrible night and a horrible room. You and your friend want your money back.

Immigration Role Play

Lesson Plan

Description - Students role play trying to get through immigration.

Preparation - Make a copy of the "Passport Sheet" for each student or have them make their own.

Warm up
Write on the board:

"Welcome to _____. May I see your passport?

What's the purpose of your visit to _____?"

Ask students where this might be said. Ask students what other questions immigration officials might ask and write them on the board.

Note - The immigration discussion questions are about immigration in general rather than going through immigration. Depending on the teacher's preference, the discussion questions can be used during the warm up, wrap up, or as a supplement if the activity runs short.

Set up
Tell students they are going to visit a lot of countries and try to get through immigration.

Give all of the students a passport sheet or have them create their own passports. They should draw a picture of themselves in the box. Explain any difficult vocabulary on the "Passport Sheet", i.e., surname, given names, difference between nationality and place of birth. After all of the students have finished their passports, divide the class in half. Choose one half to be immigration officials and tell them to put away their passport and choose the country they will be an immigration official for. Make sure no two agents have the same country. If there are an odd number of students, have an extra traveler or an extra immigration official. Remind students they should use a formal register (polite language) for the role play.

Role play
Have all the students with passports go to the front of the class. Have all of the immigration officials sit at a desk with room for the traveler to stand in front of them. Remind immigration officials that they have all the power. They decide how many questions to ask and whether or not to let someone in.

1ˢᵗ Round
Let the travelers go to the countries of their choice and try to get through immigration. When they finish getting through immigration, they should go to another country. The travelers will try to get into as many countries as they can. The immigration official decides how many questions to ask and whether to let the person through or not. After ten minutes or so, ask the travelers how many countries they were able to enter, and congratulate the student who went to the most countries.

2ⁿᵈ Round
After the 1ˢᵗ round, travelers and immigration officials switch roles. The immigration officials will pull out their passports, and the travelers will think of what country they will represent. After they switch roles, repeat the instructions from the 1ˢᵗ round.

Wrap up
After the role play, ask who was the most evil immigration official and why.

Discussion Questions

- When is immigration helpful to a country and when is harmful?

- Do you think your country needs more or less immigrants?

- What nationalities are most immigrants who come to your country?

- What would happen if we erased all country borders and let people live wherever they wanted? Would it be a good or bad thing? Why?

- Does your country have strict immigration laws? Should the laws be less strict or stricter?

- What should immigrants know before they can become citizens?

- What is the best method to slow or stop immigration? Can immigration ever be completely stopped?

- Do you think immigrants to a country work harder than people born in that country? Why or why not?

- Do you have any friends or family who are immigrants? How does that affect your view of immigration?

- How do immigrants help a country's economy?

IMMIGRATION

Passport Sheet

Passport

Surname

_____

Given Names

_____

Nationality

_____

Date of birth

_____

Place of birth

_____

Internet Role Play

Lesson Plan

Description - Students compete to win a prize for the best website idea.

Preparation - Make a copy of the "Website Idea Sheet" for each pair (optional).

Warm up

Put students into pairs. If there is an odd number, make a group of three. Ask pairs to brainstorm websites they use every day or every week. Elicit some ideas from the pairs. Now, ask them to discuss why those sites are so popular.

Note - The discussion questions are about the Internet in general rather than specifically about websites. Depending on the teacher's preference, the discussion questions can be used during the warm up, wrap up, or as a supplement if the activity runs short.

Set up

Tell pairs they will come up with a new website idea together. Tell them they will compete for a prize of $100,000 from a company that will make the website a reality. Second place will get $10,000.

Give each pair a copy of the "Website Idea Sheet", if you are using it. Give students time to come up with a website idea and fill in the sheet.

When most of the pairs look like they are finished, split each pair. One student will be a judge for the competition, and one will be a contestant.

Role play

Have the students set up the desks with two desks facing each other. Have all the judges sit facing the same way so they are facing their partner, who will be the contestant. Tell judges they are judging sites based on originality, possibility for popularity, and usefulness / entertainment.

Contestants rotate clockwise so they are facing a judge who is not their partner.

1st Round

Contestants will have two minutes to pitch their website idea to the judges. After two minutes, tell contestants to rotate clockwise to the judge next to them and pitch their idea again for two minutes. Repeat this for four turns or until students get back to their partner. Have the contestants stand up at the front of the class and ask the judges which contestant they will choose. Congratulate the two contestants with the most votes.

2nd Round

After the 1st round, pairs discuss with their original partner what the contestants learned about pitching their website idea. Contestants and investors then switch roles. Repeat the instructions for the 1st round going counter clockwise this time.

Wrap up

After the role play is finished, ask the winners of each round to present details about their website idea.

Discussion Questions

- How much time do you spend on the Internet?

- What are some of the benefits of the Internet?

- What are some of the dangers of the Internet?

- How much time should children spend on the Internet?

- How has the Internet changed the world?

- What will the Internet be like in ten years?

- Are you part of any social networks like Facebook or Google+?

- When did you get your first email address?

- What is your favorite website?

- Tell your partner / group about one website you really like.

- Should the Internet be regulated or censored?

Website Idea Sheet

Website Idea

Have an idea for website? You could win $100,000!

You are going to create a new website idea and try to win $100,000.

Your website idea should be unique and original. There shouldn't be any other websites like it. It should be entertaining and / or useful. It should also have the possibility of becoming incredibly popular.

Name of the website:

What is the general idea for the website in one sentence?

_____

_____

_____

What will the website do for people?

_____

_____

_____

Why will it be popular?

_____

_____

_____

How is it different from similar websites?

_____

_____

_____

Job Interview Role Play

Lesson Plan

Description – Students interview for a job.

Preparation - Copy / cut role play cards before class. Prepare one role play card per student. Find two job advertisements online for a job that your students would be interested in.

Warm up

Divide the class into groups of four. A group of two or three can be made if necessary. Show them one of the job advertisements you prepared. Ask groups to brainstorm what questions an interviewer for this job might ask an applicant. Elicit some of the questions they brainstormed.

Note - The questions focus on jobs in general as well as job interviews. Depending on the teacher's preference, the discussion questions can be used during the warm up, wrap up, or as a supplement if the activity runs short.

Set up

This role play can be done in several ways depending on how many students you have in your class and how long you want the activity to last. You can have applicants apply for a job as a group, with one or more students being the interviewers. You can also pair students up, with one student being the applicant and one being the interviewer. To extend the role play, have applicants rotate to a different interviewer(s) after they finish with their first role play. The following instructions are for two applicants being interviewed by two interviewers at the same time.

Hand each student in the group a role play card and give them time to read it. Let the applicants know they should brainstorm qualifications that will get them the job. Let interviewers know they should brainstorm questions. Tell the class that each pair of interviewers can only choose one applicant to offer a job to.

Role play

Applicants should set up their desk facing their interviewers but with some space between them.

All groups in the class will do the role play at the same time while the teacher monitors and makes notes of common errors. Try not to interrupt or interfere with the role play unless absolutely necessary.

Give students around eight minutes to complete the role play. The role play may run short or long depending on how outgoing and confident your students are.

When one or two groups look like they are finished, give the rest of the groups one or two minutes to finish.

If you would like to extend the activity you can make the applicants rotate to a new pair of interviewers, or you can have students switch roles.

Wrap up

Ask each pair of interviewers who they chose to be their new employee.

Discussion Questions

- What is the best way to find a job?

- What are three things you must do during a job interview and three things you must never do during a job interview?

- What are some of the worst jobs you can think of?

- What are some of the best jobs you can think of?

- What is the best way for interviewers to choose the best job applicant?

- How long do you want to work?

- Is it better to be a boss or an employee? Why?

- What would be the most satisfying job for you?

- What is one of the most exciting jobs you can think of? How about one of the most boring jobs?

- What kind of job do you want to get in the future? What kind of tasks will you have to do?

- Do you think what job someone has determines who they are?

- What is the most dangerous job?

- How difficult is it to get a job in your country?

- What company is the best to work for?

JOB INTERVIEW

Role Play Cards

Role 1

The applicant

You really need a job. You will do anything to get a job.

You recently lost your job because the company you worked for went out of business. You have two children, and you are running out of money. Feel free to lie as much as you want. You can say anything you want, if you think it will help you get the job. Be creative, and try not to be caught lying. Your goal is to get a job any way that you can.

Role 2

The interviewer

You are trying to hire the best person for the job.

You are in charge of hiring a new employee for your company. You want to hire an honest and hardworking employee. You think that some of the applicants are lying about their experience and skills. Try to catch them in a lie if you can. You will be working with this person for a long time, so you want someone you can work well with. Your goal is to hire the best person for the job, preferably someone who is honest.

Manners Role Play

Lesson Plan

Description - City officials decide on whether to fine people for bad manners.

Preparation - Copy / cut role play cards before class. One role play card per student.

Warm up

Divide students into groups of three. A group of two can be made if necessary. Ask groups to come up with a list of bad manners they hate. When groups are finished, elicit some of their ideas and make a list on the board.

Note – The discussion questions are about manners in general. Depending on the teacher's preference, the discussion questions can be used during the warm up, wrap up, or as a supplement if the activity runs short.

Set up

The local city government is trying to decide on whether to fine people with bad manners and which bad manners to fine. The money from the fines would go towards improving the city.

Tell each group they are the ones who will decide which bad manners will be fined and how much the fines will be. They will use the list on the board and any more bad manners they can think of.

Hand each student in the group a role play card and give them time to read it. If you have a group of two, you can leave out role card three. Tell students they shouldn't show their group members their card. Explain any unfamiliar vocabulary from the cards, i.e., fines, limiting [something], etc. Give students time to think of arguments to support their role.

Tell the groups they will need to discuss why a bad manner should or shouldn't be fined. Then, vote on whether to fine the bad manner. They should make a list of which, if any, bad manners will be fined, as well as how much the fines will be.

Role play

Students can stay seated in a group. All groups in the class will do the role play at the same time while the teacher monitors and makes notes of common errors. Try not to interrupt or interfere with the role play unless absolutely necessary.

Give students around ten minutes to complete the role play. The role play may run short or long depending on how outgoing and confident your students are.

When one or two groups seem to have stopped debating, tell the rest of the groups they have one minute to come to a decision on the bad manners and any fines.

Wrap up

Ask each group how many bad manners they decided to fine and which bad manners they decided not to fine. Also, ask how much some of the fines for the bad manners were.

Discussion Questions

- What are some examples of bad manners in a movie?

- What are some examples of good manners on the street?

- What are some examples of bad manners you HATE?

- Do you think people are more polite or less polite now than in the past?

- Do you know someone who is often rude?

- What are some examples of how manners have changed in your country?

- How are manners different in other countries?

- How important is it to be polite to older people, even if they are rude?

- What is something that isn't considered rude but should be?

- When someone is rude in a public place, do you say something or try to ignore the person?

Role Play Cards

Role 1
Freedom!

You think that bad manners shouldn't be fined unless they hurt other people.

The state can't fine people just because they are doing something that some people don't like. It's a dangerous thing to make laws about what people can and can't do. Next, the government will be telling people what they can and can't eat or telling people what topics they can talk about. It's ridiculous. People should have the freedom to do what they want as long as they aren't hurting anyone else. You don't want to vote for fines for any of the bad manners unless the bad manners are actually hurting people.

Role 2
Fine them all!

You think people should be fined for bad manners. Rude people with bad manners make everyone's lives worse, and they should pay the price for that.

There are so many people with bad manners. They make everyone else around them uncomfortable, and they get away with it. You want to put a stop to it by fining people who have bad manners. It will make them think twice about being rude. Plus, it means more money for the city, and more polite people will make the city a nicer place to live. You want to vote to put fines on as many bad manners as you can.

Role 3
Not totally sure about the fines.

You see the pros and cons of fining bad manners. You aren't really sure it's a good idea, but it feels right.

Fining bad manners means more money for the city, but it also means limiting people's freedoms and telling them how to live their lives. You think it might be dangerous to start fining people based just on their manners because it will be easier to fine other behaviors later. But you also think that less bad manners will make the city a better place to live. Listen to arguments the other two city officials make, and decide which way to vote.

Memory Role Play

Lesson Plan

Description – Eyewitnesses must describe a person to a detective using a picture they saw.

Preparation - Copy / cut role play cards before class. You'll only need one police officer card per group. Prepare three pictures with a different individual in each picture in different settings like a coffee shop or on the street. Make sure the pictures focus on one individual.

Warm up

Divide students into groups of three. A group of two can be made if necessary. Without explaining, choose one person in each group and tell them to look away. They will be the police officer later but don't tell them that. Show the rest of the students the pictures of individuals in a store or on the street that you prepared. You can Google "man in store" or "woman on street" to find pictures. Let the students look at each of the pictures without any explanation for ten seconds, then hide them.

Now, without any explanation, have all the students discuss what they ate for lunch last week on Wednesday. This will hopefully take students' attention off the people they saw in the photos for a few moments. After groups have discussed what they ate for a while, ask some of the students how well they remembered their meals.

Note – The discussion questions focus on memory / memories in general. Depending on the teacher's preference, the discussion questions can be used during the warm up, wrap up, or as a supplement if the activity runs short.

Set up

Tell students the person they saw in the second photo killed eight people, including two children, minutes after you saw them.

Hand each student who saw the photos an eyewitness card. Hand each student who looked away, a detective role card. Give the students time to read their card. Explain any unfamiliar vocabulary from the cards.

Role play

Students should arrange their desks so the eyewitnesses are facing the detective. Groups in the class will do the role play at the same time while the teacher monitors and makes notes of common errors. Try not to interrupt or interfere with the role play unless absolutely necessary.

Give students around six minutes to complete the role play. The role play may run short or long depending on how outgoing and confident your students are.

When it looks like one or two of the groups have finished, tell the other groups they have one minute to finish up.

Wrap up

Elicit from each group some details about the suspects. After you've elicited descriptions from each group, show the class the pictures again and see how close they were.

Discussion Questions

- What is the best memory you have?

- Who was your most memorable teacher? (Bad or good)

- Do you have any strong memories linked to a particular smell?

- How do you want people to remember you?

- How good is your memory?

- What do you wish you were better at remembering?

- Are computers making our ability to remember better or worse? Give some examples.

- How much do you think memories change over time?

- Why do you think some people remember the same events differently?

- Is the ability to memorize lots of things important? Why or why not?

Role Play Cards

Role 1
Eye witness

You were brought in by the police to describe a murder suspect.

You saw someone who, just minutes after you saw them, killed eight people, including two children, and then escaped. You must describe the person as well as you can so the police can catch the murderer. The police don't have many eyewitnesses, so it's incredibly important that you give them every tiny detail you can recall. Remember, it's up to you to give a very complete picture of what the suspect looks like so they can find the killer. If you don't give them a detailed description, the murderer might never be caught.

Role 2
Detective

You are a detective. You are interviewing eyewitnesses who saw a murderer.

You are trying to catch a person who killed eight people, then escaped. Time is running out, and you need an accurate description as soon as possible so that police on the streets know who they are looking for. The most important information is the suspect's features, but their clothing and what they were doing could be important as well. Try to recall every small detail, i.e., shoe lace color, what they were drinking, etc., and try to make sure the description is accurate. If the eyewitness is uncertain, help them remember.

Features (height, hair color, eye color, skin color, hairstyle, tattoos, etc.)

_____

_____

_____

_____

Clothing

_____

_____

What were they doing

_____

_____

Movies Role Play

Lesson Plan

Description - A group of friends is trying to decide what movie to see.

Preparation - Copy / cut role play cards before class. Prepare one role play card per student. Prepare a list of movies currently in theatres (preferably with images of the movie posters). Optionally, students can look up movies currently in the theatres on their phones.

Warm up

Divide the class into groups of four. A group of three can be made if necessary. Write this question the board: "What makes you want to see a movie?" Have students discuss the question. Elicit some of the students' thoughts.

Note - The discussion questions are about movies in general. Depending on the teacher's preference, the discussion questions can be used during the warm up, wrap up, or as a supplement if the activity runs short.

Set up

Hand each student in the group a role play card and give them time to read it. If you have a group of three, you can take out one of the role cards. Tell students they shouldn't show their group members their card. Explain any unfamiliar vocabulary from the cards.

Show students the list of movies currently in theatres or have them look up a list of movies currently in theatres. Give them a little time to look over them and decide what movies they would be willing to see based on the instructions on their card.

Explain that at the end of the role play the group must decide on just one movie to see.

Role play

Students can stay seated or do their role play standing up. All groups in the class will do the role play at the same time while the teacher monitors and makes notes of common errors. Try not to interrupt or interfere with the role play unless absolutely necessary.

Give students around seven minutes to complete the role play. The role play may run short or long depending on how outgoing and confident your students are.

Once it looks like one or two of the groups are finishing up, give the other groups one or two minutes to finish their role plays and decide what movie to watch.

Wrap up

When everyone is finished, go around the class and ask groups which movie they chose and why.

Discussion Questions

- What is your favorite genre of movie?

- Who are some of your favorite actors?

- What kind of movie is best for a date?

- Do you cry during movies?

- What is the best movie you have ever seen?

- What was the scariest movie you have ever seen?

- How often do you see movies?

- Do you usually watch movies at the theater or watch them at home?

- Do you buy DVDs or download movies?

- What is the best snack to eat during a movie?

- What do people do during movies that really annoys you?

- Which is more important, acting or special effects?

- If you could make a movie, what would it be about?

- If someone made a movie of your life, what kind of movie would it be?

MOVIES

Role Play Cards

Role 1
Action movie

You want to see an action movie. You really don't want to see a kids' movie.

You really love action movies. The more action the better. You are okay with any movie as long as it has a lot of action in it. But you don't want to watch a kids' movie. They are always so childish and silly. Sometimes there is some action, but it's just not the same when it's a cartoon. Plus, they can't put in really violent action scenes because they are meant for kids. Your goal is to get everyone to see an action movie.

Role 2
Kids' movie

You want to see a kids' movie. You really don't want to see a romantic movie.

You are in the mood for a kids' movie. You want to watch something light that isn't too serious. You definitely don't want to see a romance. They are always so dramatic. Plus, they sometimes make you cry, and you don't want to be embarrassed in front of your friends. You are okay with anything as long as it isn't too serious like a romantic movie. Your goal is to get everyone to see a kid's movie.

Role 3
Comedy

You want to see a comedy. You really don't want to see an action movie.

You want something light-hearted and not serious. You just want to laugh. You don't want to see an action movie. You aren't in the mood to see a bunch of violence and killing today. You are okay with watching any movie as long as there are some jokes in it and not too much violence. You don't want to watch anything serious. Your goal is to get everyone to watch a comedy.

Role 4
Romantic movie

You want to see a romantic movie. You don't want to see a comedy.

You are really in the mood to see a romantic movie. Something really dramatic. You aren't in the mood for a silly comedy. You want something emotional. A romantic comedy might be okay if it isn't too silly, but you would prefer a dramatic love story. If there are no romantic movies, you want something serious and dramatic. Your goal is to get everyone to watch a romantic movie.

Music Role Play

Lesson Plan

Description - Students create a band and try to get gigs at music venues.

Preparation - Make a copy of the "Musician Sheet" for each student. Prepare some examples of different music genres for students to listen to (optional).

Warm up

Put students in pairs or groups of three or four. Ask them to brainstorm as many music genres as they can. Make it a competition to see which group can brainstorm the most in a set amount of time or just let them brainstorm normally. When they are finished, elicit the genres the groups came up with. Choose a few genres and ask students what makes them unique. Let students listen to the examples of genres, if you prepared them.

Next, ask students to choose one or two of their favorite bands or artists and discuss why they like them and what makes them different from other bands and artists in their genre.

Note - The discussion questions are about music in general. Depending on the teacher's preference, the discussion questions can be used during the warm up, wrap up, or as a supplement.

Set up

Tell students they are going to create a band, group, or a solo performer. They will then try to get a gig at a local venue. Go over what a gig and venue are.

Students should work individually. Give them the "Musician Sheet" and let them create their idea for a band, group, or solo performer. When they are finished or after ten minutes, divide the class into two lines facing each other. Half of the students will be musicians and the other half will be owners of venues looking for live performers. Ask the owners of venues what type of business they have (restaurant, bar, club, coffee shop, etc.). Ask them to think of, but not say, what type of music would work best in their venue. If there is an odd number of students, make two students be a team.

Role play

Rotate the students clockwise once so they know how they will be rotating. Let the owners know they will choose only one musician to hire. They have the power, so they can be harsh and demanding.

1st Round

The musicians will have three minutes to convince the venue owners to hire them. After three minutes, tell the musicians to rotate to the next venue. Repeat this for four turns or until students get back to their original partner. Then, rotate once more but don't let them start again. (This ensures that the person they just finished talking to isn't obliged to choose them.) Ask each venue owner who they chose. Congratulate the musicians with the most votes.

2nd Round

For the 2nd round, the venue owners will now be the musicians. After switching roles, repeat the instructions from the 1st round.

Wrap up

Put students back in their original groups and have them discuss which musicians from the role play they liked the most.

Discussion Questions

- Who are some of your favorite bands or artists?

- How often do you listen to music?

- When was the last time you bought a song or album?

- Where do you buy music?

- Have you ever illegally downloaded music? Do you think it is okay or not okay to download music illegally?

- What kind of music do you listen to when you want to dance?

- What kind of music do you listen to when you are sad?

- Is there a certain song or type of music that makes you really energetic?

- Do you think music is getting better or worse?

- What kind of music will your kids listen to?

- What music did your parents listen to?

- How do you feel about your country's traditional music?

- Should people try to modernize traditional music?

- How is your country's traditional music different from other countries' traditional music?

Musician Sheet

Musician

Create a band, group, or be a solo musician.

You are going to create a new musical group or a musician identity for yourself. You will then try to get hired to play music at as many venues as you can.

Be creative when thinking of your musical identity. Don't just copy an existing musician. Try to create your own unique musical identity. Remember that some venues (restaurant, bar, club, coffee shop, etc.) work well with specific genres of music.

Describe your band, group, or musician in one sentence:

_____

_____

Musician information:

- Genre: _____

- What are your performances like? (energetic, chill, etc.)

  _____

  _____

- What makes you, as a musician, special?

  _____

  _____

- Why will your music be popular?

  _____

  _____

Natural Wonders Role Play

Lesson Plan

Description – Tourists visit a natural wonder with a tour guide who has a secret.

Preparation - Copy / cut role play cards before class. Prepare one role play card per student. Find and print one picture of a natural wonder for each group of three or four. The pictures can be of the same natural wonder or different natural wonders.

Warm up

Divide students into groups of four. A group of three can be made if necessary. Each student will tell their group about the most impressive natural place they have ever visited.

Note – The discussion questions are about natural wonders in general. Depending on the teacher's preference, the discussion questions can be used during the warm up, wrap up, or as a supplement if the activity runs short.

Set up

Tell students they are going to visit a natural wonder with a tour guide. Give each group the picture of a natural wonder. Tell them the name of the natural wonder and where it is located.

Hand each student in the group a role play card and give them time to read it. If possible, hand the tour guide role card to a confident student. For groups of four, hand out an extra role three card. If you have a group of three, don't hand out an extra role three card. Tell students they shouldn't show their group members their card. Ask students to look up any unfamiliar vocabulary from the cards and let them know if they have any questions to come up and ask you. Try to avoid going over any vocabulary like "fake" or "arrested" with

the class as it might give away the secret. Give tourists time to prepare questions and the tour guide time to think about what they will say about the natural wonder.

Role play

Students can stay seated in a group or do their role play standing up.

All groups in the class will do the role play at the same time while the teacher monitors and makes notes of common errors. Try not to interrupt or interfere with the role play unless absolutely necessary.

Give students around seven minutes to complete the role play. The role play may run short or long depending on how outgoing and confident your students are.

When one or two groups seem to have finished, tell the rest of the groups they have one minute to finish up the tour.

Wrap up

Ask the groups what happened during their tour and if anything happened with their tour guide. Give groups time to discuss what happened during the role play and let the tour guide explain their role.

Discussion Questions

- What are the three most famous natural wonders in your country?

- What natural wonders are in danger from climate change?

- Should humans try to protect natural wonders? If humans protect natural wonders, are the wonders still natural?

- Have you ever been to a natural wonder?

- What makes something a natural "wonder"?

- What are three natural wonders you would like to see before you die?

- Should people be allowed to visit a natural wonder if the visitors hurt the natural wonder just by visiting it?

- Do natural phenomena, i.e., the aurora borealis, count as natural wonders? How about things like thunderstorms?

- Are natural disasters like volcanoes and earthquakes also natural wonders?

- How many countries with natural wonders can you name? Which country do you think has the most natural wonders?

- Would you rather visit natural wonders or man-made wonders?

Role Play Cards

Role 1

The tour guide

You are the tour guide. Your job is to describe the history of the natural wonder and how it was formed.

You aren't a real tour guide. You are just pretending to be one in order to get money for your family. You don't know anything about the natural wonder, so you just have to lie about everything. Don't let anyone know you aren't a real tour guide. If they find out you are a fake tour guide, you will be arrested so try to lie well and be entertaining. Keep the tourists happy and answer all their questions, even if your answers are all lies. Your goal is to fool the tourists into thinking you are a real tour guide.

Role 2

The suspicious tourist

You are a tourist at a natural wonder. Your tour guide isn't very good though. You think he might not be a real tour guide.

You are enjoying your visit to this beautiful natural wonder, but you think the tour guide is a little suspicious. They might or might not be a real tour guide. Try to ask difficult questions about the natural wonder to make the tour guide make mistakes and prove that they aren't a real tour guide. Your goal is to get the other tourist(s) to believe that your tour guide isn't real. Your second goal is to get the tour guide to admit they really aren't a tour guide.

Role 3

The tourist

You are a tourist at a natural wonder. Your tour guide is great, and the natural wonder is beautiful. You are having a great time.

You are really enjoying your trip to this natural wonder. Your tour guide seems very knowledgeable. Ask your tour guide lots of questions about the natural wonder to learn more. One of the other tourists seems a little rude though. Ignore them, and try to learn as much from your tour guide as you can. Your goal is to learn how the natural wonder was formed and the history around the natural wonder.

Neighborhoods Role Play

Lesson Plan

Description - Neighborhood association creates the bylaws for a new neighborhood.

Preparation - Copy one "Bylaws Sheet" for each group.

Warm up

Divide students into groups of four. A group of three can be made if necessary. Teach students the meaning of bylaw and explain that bylaws are the rules that people in neighborhoods have to obey, or they will be fined. Tell students that by laws are most common in suburbs. Ask groups to brainstorm what factors make a good or bad neighborhood. Ask groups what residents can do to make their neighborhood better.

Note - The discussion questions are about neighborhoods in general not just rules for neighborhoods. Depending on the teacher's preference, the discussion questions can be used during the warm up, wrap up, or as a supplement if the activity runs short.

Set up

Tell students that a new neighborhood is being built. They are part of the rules committee of the neighborhood association, and they will create the rules residents must follow if they want to live in the new neighborhood.

Tell them that the rules they create should help improve the neighborhood and the lives of the residents. They don't need to make laws for things that are already illegal, i.e., fighting, stealing, etc.

Tell them they should decide what kind of neighborhood they want to live in and then create bylaws that will help make that neighborhood a good place to live. They can be creative with the rules if they want to live in a more interesting neighborhood.

Hand each group a bylaws sheet and let them know they should create at least eight rules but that they can make more if they would like.

Explain any unfamiliar vocabulary from the bylaws sheet, i.e., prosper, residents, etc. Tell students they must make sure that everyone in the committee is happy with the rules.

Role play

All groups in the class will do the role play at the same time while the teacher monitors and makes notes of common errors. Try not to interrupt or interfere with the role play unless absolutely necessary.

Give students around seven to ten minutes to complete the role play. The role play may run short or long depending on how outgoing and confident your students are.

When one or two groups have finished their bylaws sheet, let the other groups know they have one or two minutes to finish up.

Wrap up

Have each group read out the rules for their neighborhood. After groups finish reading their rules identify any common themes that emerge.

Discussion Questions

- Did you like the neighborhood where you grew up?

- Where is the best place to eat in your city?

- Where is there a lot of crime in your city?

- What is the worst thing a neighborhood can have?

- Where is the best place to shop in your city?

- What did you like most about the neighborhood you grew up in?

- What kind of neighborhood do you want to raise your children in?

- Do you think it should be the government's responsibility to clean up neighborhoods or are the people in the neighborhood responsible for cleaning it up?

- Do you think neighborhoods are more, or less, friendly these days?

- What will neighborhoods be like in the future?

Bylaws Sheet

Bylaws

Create bylaws for a new neighborhood.

You are the rules committee of a new neighborhood association. Decide what type of neighborhood you want to live in. Then, decide what rules will help create that neighborhood. Your rules should help your neighborhood prosper and make residents happy.

_____

_____

_____

_____

_____

_____

_____

_____

_____

_____

Neighbors Role Play

Lesson Plan

Description - Neighbors have an argument about noise.

Preparation - Copy / cut role play cards before class. Prepare one role play card per student.

Warm up

Divide students into groups of three. A group of two can be made if necessary. Elicit some traits or actions that make someone a bad neighbor. Ask groups to brainstorm some more examples as a group. Ask groups for their ideas and write them on the board. Tell groups to discuss a horrible neighbor they have had or have heard about.

Note - The discussion questions are about neighbors in general not just bad neighbors. Depending on the teacher's preference, the discussion questions can be used during the warm up, wrap up, or as a supplement if the activity runs short.

Set up

Tell students they are neighbors in an apartment complex. One neighbor is very angry. Apartment 302 is between 301 and 303.

Hand each student in the group a role play card and give them time to read it. If you have a group of two, you can leave out role card three. Tell students they shouldn't show their group members their card, but they should identify which apartment number they are in.

Explain any unfamiliar vocabulary from the cards, i.e., compromise, agreement, involved etc. Give students time to think of arguments for their role.

Tell students they must find a way to resolve the conflict so that everyone is happy.

Role play

Students should stand like they are talking in the hallway of an apartment building.

All groups in the class will do the role play at the same time while the teacher monitors and makes notes of common errors. Try not to interrupt or interfere with the role play unless absolutely necessary.

Give students around seven minutes to complete the role play. The role play may run short or long depending on how outgoing and confident your students are.

When one or two groups have come to a compromise, let the other groups know they have two minutes to finish up.

Wrap up

Elicit from each group what they decided to do to keep everyone happy.

Discussion Questions

- What do you think of your neighbors?

- Is there anything your neighbors do that annoys you?

- Did you play with kids who were your neighbors when you were a kid? Do you still keep in contact with them?

- "Good fences make good neighbors." What do you think this idiom means? Do you agree?

- Do you think neighbors were friendlier to each other in the past or are they friendlier now? Is this a good or bad thing?

- Have you ever asked to borrow something from your neighbor? Has your neighbor ever borrowed anything?

- What kind of person would be the perfect neighbor? Name at least three characteristics.

- How are countries that border each other similar to neighbors?

- Do you trust your neighbors? Would you leave them a key to your house?

- Think back in your life, who was your most memorable neighbor?

Role Play Cards

Role 1

Apartment 301

You are furious with how noisy your neighbor is. You can't get any sleep.

Your neighbor's kitchen is right beside your bedroom. Your neighbor is always banging pots and making noise past midnight. They also turn up the volume on their TV late at night. It's really loud, and you can't get any sleep. You have to get up for work at 6 a.m. every day. You are really angry, and you are going over there to tell them they better keep it quiet, or they'll regret it. Think of two other annoying things your neighbor does and complain about those, too. Go and knock on your neighbor's door 302.

Role 2

Apartment 302

You work in the evening, so you don't get home until midnight.

All you want to do after you get home from work is cook yourself a nice dinner and relax with some TV. Cooking is your only hobby, and it's how you relieve stress. You need some time after work to relax. You know your neighbors are sleeping, so you try to be as quiet as possible, but the walls are really thin. You can hear everything that goes on in the other two apartments. Sometimes they are too loud, but you don't complain because you know sometimes your cooking is loud, too. When you hear a knock, go answer the door.

Role 3

Apartment 303

You want all your neighbors to get along.

You want to have a good relationship with all your neighbors. If two of the neighbors on your floor are fighting it will be uncomfortable, and they will start trying to get revenge on each other. If they start fighting it will have a bad effect on you, even if you aren't involved. Try to get your neighbors to compromise and make an agreement that will make everyone happy.

When you hear people talking in the apartment hallway, go out and talk to your neighbors.

Personality Role Play

Lesson Plan

Description - Students role play a specific personality trait, and their partners try to guess the trait.

Preparation - Copy / cut role play cards before class. Prepare one role play card per student.

Warm up

Divide students into groups of four. A group of three can be made if necessary. Elicit some personality traits and write them on the board, i.e., compassionate, cold, aloof, imaginative, easy to anger, etc. Ask groups to brainstorm some more personality traits and write them on the board. Go over their ideas, eliminating any that aren't personality traits.

Ask students to talk about someone they know who strongly exhibits one of the personality traits on the board. Tell them to give some examples of how that personality trait affects their behavior. They don't have to name the person if they don't want to.

Note - Depending on the teacher's preference, the discussion questions can be used during the warm up, wrap up, or as a supplement if the activity runs short.

Set up

Tell students they are going to role play two friends talking over lunch. One person will choose a personality trait from the board and act like they strongly exhibit that personality trait. At the end of the role play, the other person will try to guess what personality trait their friend has.

Split the groups of four into pairs and hand each student in the group a role play card. Give them time to read it. If you have an odd number of students you can make two students friends meeting a mutual friend. Explain any unfamiliar vocabulary from the cards, i.e., small talk, role play, imagination, etc. Give students time to choose a personality trait and brainstorm what to talk about.

Role play

Rotate the students once so they know how they will be rotating, i.e., each person with a strong personality type will move to their right with the last one in line going to the front.

1st Round

The friends will have two minutes to do their role play. After two minutes they will guess the personality type. The time can be lessened or added to depending on how talkative your students are. After they have guessed and found out if they are right, ask the friends with a strong personality type to choose a different personality type to role play. Repeat this for three or four turns or until students get back to their original partner.

2nd Round

For the 2nd round, the students will switch roles. The students with the strong personality types will become guessers. After switching roles, repeat the instructions from the 1st round.

Wrap up

Put students back into their groups and ask how many personality traits each student guessed right.

Discussion Questions

- Describe your personality.

- What kinds of people do you get along well with?

- What kinds of personality traits do you hate?

- How important is personality when you are choosing a spouse?

- Do all of your friends have similar personalities?

- What kind of personality traits are best for running a business?

- What kind of personality should a doctor have?

- Is your personality more similar to your mother's or father's?

- Do you think we are born with our personalities, or do we develop them because of what happens to us?

- What personality trait would you like to develop?

- Which of your personality traits would you like to lose?

PERSONALITY

Role Play Cards

Role 1

Guess the personality type.

You are meeting a friend for lunch. After the role play ends you will guess what personality trait they have.

You are meeting a friend for lunch. The last time you saw them was a week ago at a party. Talk about how the party was. Use your imagination to create details. You can also ask how they have been and what they did since you saw them last. You can talk about the restaurant where you are eating or ask any small talk questions you want. Once the teacher ends the role play, guess what personality trait your friend has.

Role 2

Role play a personality type.

You are meeting a friend for lunch. Choose a personality type, and do the role play while exaggerating the personality trait you picked.

You are meeting a friend for lunch. The last time you saw them was a week ago at a party. Talk about how the party was. Use your imagination to create details. You can also ask how they have been and what they did since you saw them last. You can talk about the restaurant where you are eating or ask any small talk questions you want. Once the teacher ends the role play, let your friend guess what personality trait you have and tell them if they are right.

Predictions Role Play

Lesson Plan

Description - A pessimist and an optimist go on a television show to discuss their predictions for the future.

Preparation - Copy / cut role play cards before class. Prepare one role play card per student. If you can show video in your class, prepare a clip of pundits on a talk show as a model for the role play.

Warm up

Divide the class into groups of three. A group of two can be made if necessary. Write three categories on the board of areas that might change drastically in the future, i.e., energy, technology, health, government, entertainment, space, environment, etc. Ask students to brainstorm some good and bad things that might happen in the future in each category. Go over some of their ideas as a class. Elicit more categories that might change in a dramatic way in the future and write them on the board.

Note - The discussion questions focus on "will" to talk about the future. Depending on the teacher's preference, the discussion questions can be used during the warm up, wrap up, or as a supplement if the activity runs short.

Set up

Tell groups to choose three categories from the list on the board to discuss. Once groups have chosen, hand each student in the group a role play card and give them time to read it. If you have a group of two, you can use the two member group role play cards. Tell students they shouldn't show their group members their card. Explain any unfamiliar vocabulary from the cards. Show the class a clip of pundits on a talk show, if possible, to model what they will be doing.

Give students time to formulate ideas, questions, and talking points. Students can make notes if they wish.

Groups should arrange their desks or chairs to look like pundits debating on a news show. Explain that each group must discuss their predictions for each category and support their opinions. Each pundit's goal is to convince the audience that they are right and the other pundit is wrong. The host's job is to moderate the conversation and give each pundit time to talk. For the two member group, the host's job is to play devil's advocate. They should debate with the pundit and challenge their ideas.

Role play

Students can stay seated or do their role play standing up. All groups in the class will do the role play at the same time while the teacher monitors and makes notes of common errors. Try not to interrupt or interfere with the role play unless absolutely necessary.

Give students around ten minutes to complete the role play. The role play may run short or long depending on how outgoing and confident your students are. When two or three groups look like they are finished, end the role play.

Wrap up

For each group, elicit examples of good and bad things that might happen from the categories the group chose.

Discussion Questions

- Will humans ever meet aliens? What will the meeting be like?

- What kind of sci-fi movie will the future be like?

- Where will we get our energy when we run out of oil?

- Will science find a solution to the environmental problems we have? Will computers ever take over the world?

- Will we be able to add machines to our body to improve it in the future?

- How will fashion change in the future?

- Will humans ever live on another planet? When?

- How will electronics be different in 20 years?

- In 50 years there are projected to be ten billion people on the earth. How will that affect the future?

- How will medicine and health care change in the future?

- Where will you be and what will you be doing in ten years?

- What is something that will happen in the future that you are looking forward to?

- How will you change the world?

PREDICTIONS

Role Play Cards

Role 1
The optimist

You are a guest on a TV show. Your goal is to convince the people watching that your predictions about the future in each category are correct.

You believe the future is going to be amazing. Humans will come together and work together to make a better future for everyone. You think people who talk about how bad things will be are just afraid of the future and are holding humanity back. Your goal is to convince everyone that the future is going to be great and that everyone should work together to make progress for a better future.

Role 2
The pessimist

You are a guest on a TV show. Your goal is to convince the people watching that your predictions about the future in each category are correct.

You believe the future is going to be much worse than the present. You think we are heading towards the end of humans. The future will be terrible unless we are very careful, but humans might have made too many mistakes already. It might be too late to stop the disasters that are coming. You think that people who talk about progress and how great things will be are dangerous for humanity. We need to slow down progress or humans might go extinct.

Role 3
The host

You are the host of a TV show. You are recording a show with two guests who have different views about the future.

You want to be fair and balanced. You want to give both of your guests time to say their opinions, but remember you are in control of the show. You want your show to be entertaining for viewers. If one guest is talking too much, you can cut them off and get the other guest to talk. Ask questions to get the guests to talk more if you need to. You can start arguments between the guests, if you think it will improve ratings.

PREDICTIONS

Role Play Cards for Two Member Groups

Role 1
The optimist

You are a guest on a TV show. Your goal is to convince the people watching that your predictions about the future in each category are correct.

You believe the future is going to be amazing. Humans will come together and work together to make a better future for everyone. You think people who talk about how bad things will be are just afraid of the future and are holding humanity back. Your goal is to convince everyone that the future is going to be great and that everyone should work together to make progress for a better future.

Role 2
The host

You are the host of a TV show. You are recording a show with a guest who is very optimistic about the future.

You want to be fair and balanced. You want to give your audience both sides of an issue. When your guest is talking about how great the future will be, try to find problems with their predictions. Challenge your guest with other possibilities for the future. Ask your guest difficult questions so they have to defend their opinions. You are going to try to have a pessimistic view of the future to balance your guest's optimistic opinions.

Privacy Role Play

Lesson Plan

Description – Politicians debate how to vote on a new law that affects privacy.

Preparation - Copy / cut role play cards before class. Prepare one role play card per student.

Warm up

Divide students into groups of three. A group of two can be made if necessary. Ask groups to brainstorm some recent ways that people have lost privacy. Write them on the board.

Write on the board "How much do you value your privacy?" Ask groups to discuss how much privacy they are willing to give away for safety or convenience.

Note – The discussion questions are about privacy in general rather than specifically about government surveillance. Depending on the teacher's preference, the discussion questions can be used during the warm up, wrap up, or as a supplement if the activity runs short.

Set up

Tell groups a new law that will affect privacy is being debated. The new law will put high definition cameras with microphones throughout all major cities so that every public place in these cities is being watched and listened to. The video and audio will be recorded and stored for future use. This would allow police to catch any person who committed a crime in any public place and dramatically reduce crime.

They are politicians deciding how they will vote on the new law. They can choose to vote no, yes, or to amend the law. They will try to convince their fellow politicians to vote their way.

Hand each student in the group a role play card and give them time to read it. If you have a group of two, you can leave out role card three. Tell students they shouldn't show their group members their card, and they shouldn't just read the card out to the group. Explain any unfamiliar vocabulary from the cards, i.e., commit, reduction, invasion of privacy, etc. Give students time to think of arguments to support their role.

Role play

Students can stay seated in a group or do their role play standing up.

All groups in the class will do the role play at the same time while the teacher monitors and makes notes of common errors. Try not to interrupt or interfere with the role play unless absolutely necessary.

Give students around seven minutes to complete the role play. The role play may run short or long depending on how outgoing and confident your students are.

When one or two groups seem to have stopped debating, tell the rest of the groups they have one minute to come to a decision about what to do.

Wrap up

Ask each individual student how they will vote and tally the votes up for the class to see if the law will be struck down, implemented, or amended.

Discussion Questions

- Do you think websites like Facebook and other social platforms take away too much of your privacy?

- Do you think that all people have the right to privacy? How about convicted criminals?

- The only people who need privacy are people who are doing something illegal. Do you agree or disagree? Why?

- Do you think the Internet increases privacy or takes away privacy?

- What is the greatest threat to privacy?

- How private should corporations be? Should the public have access to corporate records?

- How transparent should a government be?

- Where do you like to go when you want to be alone?

- Should there be more, or less, security cameras around cities?

- How is privacy viewed in your culture?

PRIVACY

Role Play Cards

Role 1
Freedom

You think everyone should vote no on the new law. The government shouldn't be spying on its citizens every time they leave their houses.

People should be allowed to walk freely in public without being watched and listened to. This law would make people feel like they have to think before they say anything or do anything because someone is watching and listening. What's next? Having a law that requires a camera in every room of every house to prevent crimes in homes and using people's phones to record their conversations at all times? It's a dangerous first step. If we give up freedom for safety we will have neither. Convince everyone to vote no.

Role 2
Safety

You think everyone should vote yes to the new law. With all the cameras and audio recordings we can greatly reduce crime.

If we have high quality audio and video throughout every city we can reduce crime down to almost nothing. If criminals know they are always being watched and listened to, they won't commit crimes. Think of all the lives that will be saved and the reduction in crime. We must put these cameras up, or we are allowing people to be killed, beaten, and robbed. People want safety, and this law will give it to them. If people aren't doing anything wrong they don't have anything to be afraid of. Convince everyone to vote yes.

Role 3
No audio, limited video

You think everyone should vote to amend the law. You want to amend the law to only include video in high crime areas, but not audio.

Cameras in high crime areas will definitely reduce crime. We don't need them everywhere. We can use the cameras to identify criminals, track them, and arrest them. But putting high quality audio on the cameras is too much. People shouldn't have to worry that the government is listening to everything they say. The cameras in high crime areas should be enough. We don't need the audio, too. It's too much of an invasion of privacy. Convince everyone to amend the law.

Selling Role Play

Lesson Plan

Description - Students try to sell something they have to a customer.

Preparation - Make a copy of the "Product Sheet" for each student (optional). Prepare a picture of a useless or ridiculous object.

Warm up

Put students in pairs or groups of three or four. Ask them to brainstorm some tricks that advertisers use to sell products. Elicit some of their ideas. Next, ask students brainstorm how they would sell the useless or ridiculous object in the picture. Elicit some of their ideas as to how to sell it.

Note - The discussion questions are about selling in general. Depending on the teacher's preference, the discussion questions can be used during the warm up, wrap up, or as a supplement.

Set up

Tell students they are going to try to sell something that they own (not their cellphone). They'll need to convince someone to buy it. Their goal will be to sell to as many people as possible and make as much money as possible.

Students should work individually. Give them the "Product Sheet" if you are using it. Otherwise, let them use their own paper to write notes.

When they are finished, or after five minutes, divide the class into two lines facing each other. Half of the students will be sellers and the other half will be buyers. If there is an odd number of students, make two students be a team.

Role play

Rotate the students once so they know how they will be rotating, i.e., each seller moves to their right with the last one in line going to the front. Let the buyers know they will choose only one product to buy. They have the power, so they can be harsh and demanding. Remind buyers and sellers that sellers can lie all they want to sell their product. Their only goal is to sell as many products as they can and make the most money they can.

1st Round

The seller will have three minutes to convince the buyer to buy their product. After three minutes, tell the sellers to rotate to the next buyer. Repeat this for four turns or until students get back to their original partner. Then, rotate once more but don't let the role play start again. (This ensures that the person they just finished talking to isn't obliged to choose them.) Ask each buyer which product they bought, how much it was, and why they bought it. Congratulate the sellers that sold the most and made the most money.

2nd Round

For the 2nd round, the buyers will now be the sellers. After switching roles, repeat the instructions from the 1st round.

Wrap up

Put students back in their original groups and have them discuss the strategies for selling products that worked best. Elicit some of the groups' opinions.

Discussion Questions

- When was the last time you sold something? What was it?

- Do you consider yourself a good salesperson? Why or why not?

- What is the most important personality trait for a salesperson to have?

- Do you think selling is an art form? Why or why not?

- Has anyone sold you something that you regretted buying?

- Have you ever lied when selling something?

- What are some of the most annoying things companies do to sell products?

- How often do you buy or sell used things?

- Where is the best place to sell things you don't want any more?

- Do you think that a salesperson could sell you something you didn't want to buy? Why or why not?

Product Sheet

Product Sheet

Try to sell one of your possessions as a product.

Choose something you have with you but not your cellphone. You will try to sell this item to as many people as you can.

Your goal is to make as much money as you can and sell your product to as many people as possible. Remember, you can lie as much as you want to sell your product.

Your product:

- What is it? _____

- Why should someone buy it? How will it help them?

  _____

  _____

  _____

- What makes your product different from similar products?

  _____

  _____

  _____

- What are some reasons people might not want to buy it?

  _____

  _____

  _____

Single Life Role Play

Lesson Plan

Description - Single friends try to stop their friend from getting married.

Preparation - Copy / cut role play cards before class. Prepare one role play card per student.

Warm up

Divide students into groups of three. A group of two can be made if necessary. Ask groups to brainstorm the pros and cons of single life and write them on the board. Go over their ideas as a class.

Note - The discussion questions are about single / married life in general. Depending on the teacher's preference, the discussion questions can be used during the warm up, wrap up, or as a supplement if the activity runs short.

Set up

Tell students they are friends, and they are meeting for lunch. One of them has some big news.

Hand the most confident student the "Getting married!" card and hand the single card to the rest of the group members. Tell students they shouldn't show their group members their card or talk about their role.

Explain any unfamiliar vocabulary from the cards, i.e., partner in the sense of a gender neutral way of saying boyfriend / girlfriend, etc.

Give students time to think of arguments for their role.

Role play

The two single friends should sit. Tell the student with the "Getting married!" card (without saying that they are getting married) to stand and join the group when the role play starts.

All groups in the class will do the role play at the same time while the teacher monitors and makes notes of common errors. Try not to interrupt or interfere with the role play unless absolutely necessary.

Start the role play and give students around seven minutes to complete the role play. The role play may run short or long depending on how outgoing and confident your students are.

When one or two groups look like they are finished, let the other groups know they have one minute to finish up.

Wrap up

Elicit from each "Getting married!" student whether they changed their mind or if they are still getting married.

Discussion Questions

- What are some of the differences between married life and single life? Are the differences the same for men and women?

- Are you single or in a relationship? Do you wish you had a different relationship status?

- Why do some people choose to remain single?

- Who are some famous people who are single?

- Are there more single people in the city or the countryside?

- Are most of your friends married or single?

- Do you ever try to set your single friends up on dates?

- How do your habits change when you are single versus when you are in a relationship?

- Do you have any friends who love being single or who can't stand being single?

Role Play Cards

Role 1
Getting married!

You are going to ask your longtime partner to marry you.

You can't wait to tell your friends the good news. You bought a ring, and you are going to propose to your partner. You've loved them for a long time, and you think it's finally time to get married and start a life together. Your partner is your perfect other half, and you will make a great married couple. You've been wanting to get married for a long time, and now is the right time. You never want to go back to being single. Your friends are going to be really happy for you.

Role 2
Single

You are single and loving it.

Your friend said they have some big news. You expect that your friend is going to propose, but you hope not. Their partner is all wrong for them. You think your friend should dump them, not marry them. They make a terrible match. If they get married they are going to be miserable. Plus, your friend already spends all their time with their partner. If they get married, you may never see your friend again. Do whatever you can to convince your friend to dump their partner and be single like you.

Super Heroes Role Play

Lesson Plan

Description - Students pitch a super hero movie idea to studio executives.

Preparation - Copy one "Movie Idea Sheet" for each group (optional).

Warm up

Put students in groups of two for small classes or groups of four for larger classes. Groups of three can be made if necessary. Elicit some super heroes or villains they know and their super powers. Next, tell groups to create three super heroes or super villains. They'll need to create a name and super powers for each hero / villain. Elicit some of the groups' ideas for heroes and villains.

Note - The discussion questions are about super heroes in general, not just super hero movies. Depending on the teacher's preference, the discussion questions can be used during the warm up, wrap up, or as a supplement if the activity runs short.

Set up

Explain unfamiliar vocabulary, i.e., pitch, movie studio, studio executives, plot etc.

Tell groups they are going to pitch a new super movie idea to studio executives. They can use the super heroes they have already created or create new ones, but they can only use super heroes / villains they created. Give groups a "Movie Idea Sheet" if you are using it. Give groups time to come up with an idea for a super hero movie.

When they are finished, or after ten minutes, divide each group in half. Half of the students will be pitching the idea, and the other half will be studio executives. Set up the desks so the studio executives are facing the students who are pitching the movie. Studio executives should quickly decide on a name for their movie studio.

Role play

Rotate the students pitching their ideas clockwise so they know how they will be rotating and so they are facing new studio executives. Let the studio executives know they will choose only one movie to make.

1st Round

The students pitching their idea will have three minutes to convince the studio executives to make their movie. After three minutes, tell the students pitching ideas to rotate clockwise to the next studio executive. Repeat this for four turns or until students get back to their original partner. Then, rotate once more but don't let them pitch their idea. (This ensures that the executives they just finished talking to aren't obliged to choose them.) Ask each studio executives to choose the one show they will make. Congratulate the students with the most popular movie ideas.

2nd Round

For the 2nd round, the students pitching ideas will now be the studio executives. After switching roles, repeat the instructions from the 1st round but rotate counter clockwise.

Wrap up

Put students back in their original groups and have them discuss the best movie ideas they heard.

Discussion Questions

- Who is your favorite super hero? Why?

- What super power would you like to have?

- If you had super powers would you be a super hero or a super villain?

- Do you prefer dark super heroes like Batman or purely good super heroes like Superman? Why?

- Does a person's favorite super hero tell you anything about their personality? What does your favorite super hero say about your personality?

- Are there any real super heroes?

- What is your favorite super hero movie?

- Why have super hero movies become so popular?

- Do you think comic books are good or bad for children?

- How have super heroes changed over the years?

Movie Idea Sheet

Movie Idea

A great new super hero movie

You are going to create an idea for a new super hero movie. You'll then try to convince studio executives to make your movie.

Be creative when coming up with your super hero movie. You'll need to make all new super heroes so studios won't have to pay a comic company to make the movie. But remember, you'll have to convince the executives that it will be profitable.

Movie information:

- Title: _____

- Super hero(es) and their power(s):

  _____

  _____

  _____

- Super villain(s) and their power(s):

  _____

  _____

  _____

- Plot:

  _____

  _____

  _____

Technology Role Play

Lesson Plan

Description - A salesperson is trying to convince two reluctant shoppers to buy a new piece of technology.

Preparation - Copy / cut role play cards before class. Prepare one role play card per student. Research a brand new gadget to tell the class about. Include pictures and a video if possible.

Warm up

Present the new piece of tech you researched. Show students pictures and a video of if possible. Divide students into groups of three. A group of two can be made if necessary. Go over some reasons why it's such an amazing new piece of tech and the details of the product, including the price. Ask students to brainstorm some reasons why people should and shouldn't buy the new gadget. Go over some of their ideas as a class. Ask groups to brainstorm some reasons why some people don't like adopting new technologies. Go over some of their ideas as a class.

Note - The discussion questions are about technology in general. Depending on the teacher's preference, the discussion questions can be used during the warm up, wrap up, or as a supplement if the activity runs short.

Set up

Hand each student in the group a role play card and give them time to read it. If you have a group of two you can leave out one of the customer role cards.

Tell students they shouldn't show their group members their card. Explain any unfamiliar vocabulary from the cards.

Give customers time to think of reasons they don't want to buy the gadget you told them about. Give the salesperson time to look up

sales material on their phone. They will try to convince the other group members to buy the new piece of technology.

After they have prepared, move the customers to another group, if you have more than one group. This puts the sales person and customers in a more natural dynamic.

Extension - If you have more than one group, you can get the groups to research a new bit of tech together on their phones before moving the customers to a new group.

Role play

Students can stay seated. All groups in the class will do the role play at the same time while the teacher monitors and makes notes of common errors. Try not to interrupt or interfere with the role play unless absolutely necessary.

Give students around eight minutes to complete the role play. The role play may run short or long depending on how outgoing, confident, or argumentative your students are.

Once it looks like one or two groups are slowing down or are finished, end the role play.

Wrap up

Ask each salesperson how many sales they made. If any of the customers changed their mind, ask them why they changed their mind.

TECHNOLOGY

Discussion Questions

- Talk about how technology has changed in your lifetime.

- What do you think has been the most important new invention in the last 100 years?

- Are there any new gadgets that you really want to get?

- What do you think will be the next biggest technological advance?

- How can countries help to create more inventors?

- What is your favorite piece of technology you own?

- How will computers change in the future?

- Do you think there will be more or less new innovation in the future?

- Is there a piece of technology that you really want that doesn't exist?

- Give some examples of technology that have made the world worse.

- What do you think is the most important thing humans have created?

- Do you think people will travel outside of our solar system? How will they get there?

- Do you like new gadgets or do you prefer to use technology you are comfortable with?

- What are the possibilities of technology in clothing?

- What is the future of transportation?

TECHNOLOGY

Role Play Cards

Role 1
The salesperson

You are a tech salesperson. You make commission on every sale you make. You really need to make a lot of sales this week to pay for your child's surgery.

You have to make as many sales as you can this week to help pay for the surgery your child is going to have. Try to convince the customers to buy as much as they can. You can even bend the truth a little bit. Remember, you can try to sell them more than one as gifts for their family. Your goal is to sell more than anyone else.

Role 2
Reluctant customer

You are a customer who is talking to a salesperson. You are interested in what they are selling, but you are reluctant to buy it.

You think that it's bad to buy new electronics every year and throw away perfectly good older gadgets. It wastes money and is bad for everyone but the companies. You really don't want to be one of those people who always buys the newest tech and then throws it away when the next big thing comes out, but you really love new technology. You know you shouldn't buy it, but you want it. Try to resist the urge to buy.

Role 3
Curious customer

You are a customer who is talking to a salesperson. You aren't interested in buying what they are selling, but you want to know why it's so popular.

You really don't care about new technology. You believe that things were better before all these new gadgets came out. You don't keep up with tech news, but you've heard a lot about this new gadget. You are interested in learning more about it, but you don't want to buy it. Your goal is to get more information about the product and understand why everyone loves it so much but not to buy it.

Television Role Play

Lesson Plan

Description - Students create a TV show concept and try to get it accepted by TV network executives.

Preparation - Make a copy of the "TV Show Idea Sheet" for each student (optional).

Warm up

Put students in pairs or groups of three or four. Ask them to brainstorm some of the most popular English language TV shows out now. Elicit the shows and write them on the board. Next, ask students to pick one or two shows and talk about why they are popular. Elicit some of their ideas as to why the shows are so popular.

Note - The discussion questions are about television in general. Depending on the teacher's preference, the discussion questions can be used during the warm up, wrap up, or as a supplement.

Set up

Tell students they are going to create an idea for a new television show. They'll then need to convince TV network executives to make the show.

Students should work individually. Give them the "TV Show Idea Sheet" if you are using it. Otherwise, let them use their own paper to write notes.

When they are finished, or after ten minutes, divide the class into two lines facing each other. Half of the students will be show creators, and the other half will be network executives. If there is an odd number of students, make two students be a team.

Role play

Rotate the students once so they know how they will be rotating, i.e., each show creator will move to their right with the last one in line going to the front. Let the TV network executives know they will choose only one show to make. They have the power, so they can be harsh and demanding.

1st Round

The show creators will have three minutes to convince the network executive to make their show. After three minutes, tell the show creators to rotate to the next television network executive. Repeat this for four turns or until students get back to their original partner. Then, rotate once more but don't let them pitch their idea. (This ensures that the person they just finished talking to isn't obliged to choose them.) Ask each network executive to choose the one show they will make. Congratulate the two show creators who received the most votes.

2nd Round

For the 2nd round, the show creators will now be the network executives. After switching roles, repeat the instructions from the 1st round.

Wrap up

Put students back in their original groups and have them discuss which shows they would most like to watch.

Discussion Questions

- About how many hours of TV do you watch every day?

- What are some of your favorite shows?

- Do you like any foreign TV shows?

- What is the funniest show on television?

- Do you think people watch too much television?

- Are TV shows getting better or worse?

- Would you like to be on TV?

- Do you have a favorite channel?

- Do you have cable, satellite television, or neither?

- Can you recommend a TV show to your classmates?

- What is the best drama on TV now?

TV Show Idea Sheet

TV Show Idea

Create an idea for a new TV show.

You are going to create a new idea for a TV show. You'll then have to convince TV network executives to make your show.

Be creative when thinking of your TV show idea but remember you will need to convince TV network executives that your show will be popular and profitable.

Describe your show idea in one sentence:

_____

_____

_____

Show information:

- Genre: _____

- Characters:

  _____

  _____

- Similar shows:

  _____

  _____

- Why it will be popular:

  _____

  _____

Travel Role Play

Lesson Plan

Description - Friends try to decide where to go on vacation.

Preparation - Copy / cut role play cards before class. Prepare one role play card per student. Find pictures of countries students might want to travel to (optional).

Warm up

Show pictures of different countries or elicit the names of countries and write them on the board. Divide students into groups of three. A group of two can be made if necessary. Ask students to brainstorm some reasons why someone would want to take a vacation in each of the countries. Go over some of their ideas as a class.

Note - The discussion questions are about travel in general. Depending on the teacher's preference, the discussion questions can be used during the warm up, wrap up, or as a supplement if the activity runs short.

Set up

Hand each student in the group a role play card and give them time to read it. If you have a group of two, you can leave out role card three. Tell students they shouldn't show their group members their card. Explain any unfamiliar vocabulary from the cards. Give students time to think of places they want to go based on their card. Each student will choose a country they want to go to for a vacation. They will try to convince the other group members to go to the country they picked.

Explain that each group must choose ONE country they will all go to. If they have time, they should also choose the activities they will do in that country.

Note - The teacher can decide whether to allow students to use their phones to research possible countries to go to.

Role play

Students can stay seated or do their role play standing up. All groups in the class will do the role play at the same time while the teacher monitors and makes notes of common errors. Try not to interrupt or interfere with the role play unless absolutely necessary.

Give students around ten minutes to complete the role play. The role play may run short or long depending on how outgoing and confident your students are.

Once every group has chosen a country and a few groups have talked about the activities they want to do, end the role play.

Wrap up

Elicit the countries each group chose and why they chose that country. Elicit some of the activities they want to do in the country.

Discussion Questions

- Where would you like to go on vacation?

- Tell your partner about your best travel story.

- What are some things you always take with you on a trip?

- Do you prefer package tours or making your own trip?

- Where did you spend your last vacation? What did you do?

- What are some of the benefits of travelling alone?

- What are some of the benefits of travelling with a group?

- What is the longest journey you have ever made?

- Do you prefer to travel to places with lots of tourists or places without many other tourists? Why?

- How do you think travel improves a person?

Role Play Cards

Role 1

City and culture vacation

You and your friends are going on a two week vacation. Everyone needs to agree on one place to go.

You can't wait to go on vacation with your friends. This time you are going to a big city to experience culture and do some shopping. Last vacation you went hiking with your friends. It was dirty and hard, and you had a horrible time. Two years ago you convinced everyone to go to Rome, and everyone had a great time. You want another vacation like that. You really want to walk around a beautiful city and experience its culture.

Role 2

Nature adventure vacation

You and your friends are going on a two week vacation. Everyone needs to agree on one place to go.

You are really excited about going on vacation with your friends. Last year you convinced everyone to go on an amazing hike through Patagonia. Everyone had a really great time, so you are going to convince them again to go on an adventure vacation. You really want to get out into nature, do some hiking, and be as active as possible.

Role 3

Relaxing beach vacation

You and your friends are going on a two week vacation. Everyone needs to agree on one place to go.

You have been really stressed lately, but your vacation is coming soon. You are really looking forward to going on a relaxing beach vacation with your friends. Your friends chose where to go for the last two vacations, so this year it's your turn to choose where to go for vacation. You only want to relax with your friends on a beach and get rid of some stress.

Wonders (Human Made) Role Play

Lesson Plan

Description - Government officials must come up with ideas for a wonder their country will create.

Preparation – Copy / cut role play cards before class. Optionally, gather some examples of human made wonders. Googling "Civilization wonders" will come up with a good list to choose from.

Warm up

Divide students into groups of three (a group of two can be made if necessary). Show them some examples of human made wonders or elicit some from the groups. Make sure to include some modern wonders. Groups then brainstorm more human made wonders and write them on the board.

Note -The discussion questions are general questions about human made wonders not just about modern wonders. Depending on the teacher's preference, the discussion questions can be used during the warm up, wrap up, or as a supplement if the activity runs short.

Set up

Tell students that their country's government is planning to build a new wonder of the world. They are government officials who come up with a recommendation for what to build.

Hand each student in the group a role play card and give them time to read it. If you have a group of two you can leave out role card three. Tell students that they shouldn't show their group members their card. Explain any unfamiliar vocabulary from the cards (quarantine, lethal / non-lethal force, etc.). Give students about three or four minutes to individually brainstorm wonders that could be built that will achieve the goal on their card.

Once students have had time to brainstorm alone, start the role play.

Remind them that the group must decide on only one wonder to recommend to the government.

Role play

Students should arrange their desks so that they are facing each other. All groups in the class will do the role play at the same time while the teacher monitors and makes notes of common errors. Try not to interrupt or interfere with the role play unless absolutely necessary.

Give students around eight minutes to complete the role play. The role play may run short or long depending on how outgoing and confident your students are.

When one or two groups have come to a decision let the other groups know that they have two minutes to finish up.

Optional extension – Have students draw their wonder on paper.

Wrap up

Have each group present their wonder to the class. After all the groups have presented, vote on which wonder should be chosen. Groups can't vote for their wonder.

WONDERS (Human Made)

Discussion Questions

- How many of the seven ancient wonders can you name? How many are left?

- 100 million votes were cast for the new human wonders of the world, the new seven wonders are: Chichén Itzá in Mexico, Christ the Redeemer in Brazil, The Great Wall in China, Machu Picchu in Peru, Petra in Jordan, The Roman Colosseum in Italy, The Taj Mahal in India

- Have you been to any of them or do you know someone who has been to one of them?

- What do you know about each one?

- Which ones would you like to go to?

- Why do you think people voted for these wonders?

- Are there any you would add to this list of human made wonders?

- Can you think of any wonders made in the last 50 years?

- What are some of the human made wonders of your country?

- Do you think it is a good idea for governments to fund "wonders" for their countries? Why or why not?

- Which would you prefer to see, human wonders or natural wonders? Why?

WONDERS (Human Made)

Role Play Cards

Role 1
Show of Power

You want to build a wonder that will show the world your country's power.

You want the wonder that your government to be so spectacular that other countries will be amazed by the power of your country. The new wonder of the world should fill people with awe or fear. You want to show the rest of the world that your country is incredibly powerful. It doesn't have to be useful but it should make people pay attention to your country. Money shouldn't matter because this wonder is about proving your country's worth to the world.

Role 2
Tourism

You want to build a wonder that will bring a lot of tourists to your country.

You want the new world wonder to be a magnet for tourists. It should be something that people want to visit. It should be a new symbol for your country. The wonder should bring in lots of money and improve the economy of your country. If it brings in enough tourists it will more than pay for itself and will bring money to your country for many years to come. The wonder should be bring in more money than it costs so it doesn't hurt your country's economy.

Role 3
For the Citizens

You want to build a wonder that will help the citizens of your country.

The new wonder that your country is planning to build should benefit the citizens of your country. It should be useful and make the lives of the people in your country better. It's great if it pulls in tourists that help the local economy. But the tourists shouldn't be allowed to make the local people's lives worse. This wonder should be all about improving the lives of citizens, not be a show of power or a magnet for tourists. It's the government's job to make the lives of people living in the country better.

Topic Index

TOPIC INDEX

WHAT'S NEXT

Looking for more?

We at ECQ publishing have a lot to offer ESL / EFL teachers. Here is some more information about what we are doing and how you can get involved.

Check out our other books

We have lots of books for ESL / EFL teachers. You can find out about our other books on our website (*eslconversationquestions.com*).

ESL Worksheets and Activities for Kids

500 Grammar Based Conversation Questions

1000 Conversation Questions: Designed for use in the ESL or EFL Classroom

IELTS Study Guide: Quick Tips, Tricks, and Strategies

You can purchase all of our books on Amazon or at select online book stores. Ask your local book store if they carry our books. If they don't, they can usually order them for you.

Leave a review on Amazon

Every review makes a big difference. Reviews help other teachers find our books on Amazon. So if you think this book can help others, let them know on Amazon. I really appreciate it!

Plus if you leave a review, you can join our review club and get free review copies of our new books and other books in our growing collection. You can find out more in the extras section at the beginning of the book.

Join our reviewer program

We are always looking for qualified reviewers for our books.

So if you leave a review of this book and are interested in receiving a free digital copy of one of our books as a review copy, let me know which of the reviews is yours and which book you are interested in at:

larrypitts@eslconversationquestions.com

We only ask that you actually review the review copy we send you. Once you write a review of the book we sent you, we can send you a digital review copy of another one of our books.

We'll also send you a review copy of any new books we release.

Questions, suggestions, or problems?

I love hearing feedback from readers. If you have any questions I would be happy to answer them. If you have suggestions for this book or a suggestion for a new book I would love to hear about them.

Also, if you have any problems or if you noticed any mistakes I would love to hear about them so I can fix them as soon as possible.

You can reach me by email: *larrypitts@eslconversationquestions.com*

Made in United States
Troutdale, OR
10/12/2024

23711299R00093